The Keys to NTI:

An Abridged Version of
The Holy Spirit's Interpretation
of the New Testament

Edited by Regina Dawn Akers

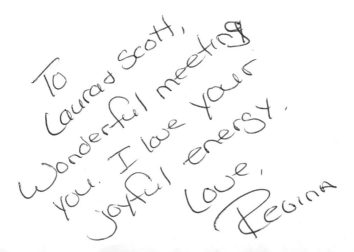

To Conrad Scott,
Wonderful meeting
you. I love your
joyful energy.
Love,
Regina

Other works by Regina Dawn Akers

The Holy Spirit's Interpretation of the New Testament (NTI),
published by O Books of London,
available from www.amazon.com

*The Holy Spirit's Interpretation of the New Testament (NTI) –
AUDIO CDs,*
available from www.diamondclearvision.com

*The Holy Spirit's Interpretation of the New Testament (NTI) –
AUDIO download,*
available from www.audiblespirit.com

The Teachings of Inner Ramana – Book with Audio CDs
available from diamondclearvision.com

The Teachings of Inner Ramana – AUDIO download
available from www.audiblespirit.com

The Keys to NTI:

An Abridged Version of
the Holy Spirit's Interpretation of
the New Testament

Foundation for the Holy Spirit

Scripture taken from the HOLY BIBLE, NEW INTERNATIONAL VERISION. Copyright © 1973, 1978, 1984 International Bible Society. Used by permission of Zondervan Bible Publishers.

ISBN: 978-0-9846874-6-6

Published and distributed by *Diamond Clear Vision*

140 Adams St.

Quincy, MA 02169

www.diamondclearvision.com

Email - info@diamondclearvision.com

- - - - -

If you are unable to order this book from your local bookseller, you may order directly from the publisher. Special quantity discounts for organizations are available.

Cover Art by

Abigail Parkhurst & Melissa Yoes,

www.HoneybeeGraphics.com

Printed by Shanghai KS Printing Co., China

The Keys to NTI:
An Abridged Version

This is an abridged version of "The Holy Spirit's Interpretation of the New Testament: A Course in Understanding and Acceptance," also known as NTI (New Testament interpretation). NTI is a metaphysical interpretation that points to non-dualism or oneness as divine truth. It was received from within by an average woman who read the Bible after asking for truth to be revealed to her. She promised to release what she had been taught to believe in order to learn what God would have her know.

NTI is a teaching about our one divine Self. It helps us realize Self by pointing out obstacles to that realization and by providing simple practices that help us transcend those obstacles. Many people find NTI helpful and easy to understand. However, no teaching is for everyone. This abridged version is provided as a sampling of the wisdom taught in NTI. It is made available to help you discover if NTI is right for you. The chapters in this version are the chapters most often called "favorites" by students of NTI. We simply call them "the keys."

Contents

NTI Luke, Chapter 1

(v 1 – 4) This book was written in love and given with the blessings of true discovery. In this way, the book is filled with the opportunity for discovery. We may open up to its power and discover our truth together.

(v 5 – 56) Each one comes to the awareness of truth from where he is, so where he is, is where he must begin to learn. There is no shame in his starting point, wherever that starting point seems to be.

The book of Luke begins with the story of ordinary people at different points in their lives. They have been judged as good by the writer of the book, but this judgment is irrelevant. For if it was their goodness that made them worthy of the Holy Spirit, others could be judged as unworthy, and this is impossible. Each one is worthy, and each one has received the Holy Spirit. There are no differences among men. All are loved as precious; all are cared for; all receive guidance; and all are called to return to the Lord. The form of their calling and their path may seem different, but its purpose is the same.

You who are reading this are blessed, for you are beloved beyond measure. You are the treasure that is sought. You are everything, complete in God. The Holy Spirit is born in you. His kingdom is within your awareness, for His kingdom is your kingdom. You, dear one, are the One. Together, we will learn this lesson. Amen.

📖(v 57 – 80) Listening and follow-through are key to discovery of blessings that already are. This is what is symbolized through the story of John's birth. His mother heard the thought of the Holy Spirit. When the time came to follow-through, she remembered the thought, and chose it again.

Within the story, Elizabeth's decision to follow guidance was not understood by others. They urged her to make another choice. This is how it will be with you, but understand where the struggle comes from, that you may resist temptation to ignore your guidance.

Within your mind, there is a belief that is in opposition to God. This belief does not seem sinful to you, and so you do not recognize it as the basis of sin.

The belief that leads to this confusion is the belief that you are a separate entity. It is the belief that there is a *you* and a *them*. It is the belief that there is a *you* and that there is a universe of objects that are separate from you. This belief you accept as a fact and you do not question it, so it does not occur to you that it is a mistaken belief that can be given up.

This belief has a voice within your mind. Its voice you call *your thoughts*. Only because you do not question this belief, you do not question these thoughts that you claim as yours. If you did question them, you would see that they are not loving thoughts. Close examination would reveal that they are based on the belief that there is something inherently wrong with you as a separate entity. These thoughts doubt your worth, and in fact, *they deny your worth entirely*.

Thoughts that deny your worth also deny the Voice of Worth, which is the Holy Spirit. This is why you will find great temptation to choose against your guidance. Realize the source of this temptation and it will be helpful to you. For when you do not realize the source of temptation, you are easily tricked into listening to the thoughts of your unworthiness.

In this story, Zechariah represents the answer of faith. Faith is a peaceful choice that trusts your worth must be true. Therefore, it chooses the Voice of Worth over the voice of worthlessness. This is what Zechariah did in choosing to follow the voice of his wife over the voice of his friends. This is a choice you can make consistently without fail, because you *are Worth*, and so you are worthy to choose the Voice of Worth.

NTI Luke, Chapter 2

📖(v 1 – 20) The birth of Jesus represents the birth of willingness, humble at first, but promising within it all of

the glory of Heaven. Mary pondered this promise in her heart, not with the worrisome thoughts of the ego, but *in her heart* where the Holy Spirit is.
This is what I ask of you:

> *Willingness has been born in the mind. This willingness promises all of the glory of Heaven, for this willingness is the savior, the Christ, and it is with you within your heart. Do not worry how this willingness will grow to become the glory it promises to be. Rest, instead, with the thought of the promise, and be grateful. It is through your love and gratitude that this babe is nursed. Its growth is inevitable, so do not worry about it. Love it in your heart, and be happy there.*

📖(v 21 – 40) We see through the story of Jesus' consecration at the temple that this symbol of willingness has been blessed by the Holy Spirit. This tiny willingness, only newly born and without achievement of any kind, is received by the Holy Spirit as a wonderful gift, and it is received with eternal gratitude.

So it is with *your* willingness, no matter how humble that willingness may seem to be to you. It is the willingness the Holy Spirit has waited for, and it is this willingness for which the Holy Spirit sings praises unto you.

Through this willingness, thoughts of deception will be revealed through the grace of the Holy Spirit. Deception shall be seen as deception, and truth shall be seen as truth. All of the angels in Heaven shall rejoice because of you.

(v 41 – 52) There will be conflict in your mind as this young willingness grows within you. Sometimes your goal may seem lost to you, and you will forget your focus and return to the focus of the world. But never fear. The willingness has been born and cannot be lost. It is within the temple of your heart, forever safe, clear in understanding, paving your way for you. When you forget your willingness and then remember it, return to it there in your heart. You will find it there, safe within your Father's Love, growing in strength, sure of who it is.

Rejoice, for your willingness cannot be lost.

Rejoice, for you cannot make a mistake that will cause you to lose your willingness. It is always there, waiting patiently and lovingly for your return to it. When you forget, just return again. And then we shall continue on together. Nothing is ever lost. Nothing is taken away.

NTI Luke, Chapter 3

📖(v 1 – 20) Your willingness is the calling within you. This willingness is within everyone, resting patiently within the heart, waiting for the day it is asked to sing its song. The song it sings is a calling, asking the one who hears its tune to follow it to a new way and a new day.

John the Baptist is the symbol of this calling within all of us. Not yet fully the Christ, it is the voice within a split mind that calls it to return to one mind, which is the Christ. For Christ is free of illusions and released from distractions, singularly focused on the willingness that is the Will of God.

What distracts *you* from the singular thought of God?

Distractions take many forms. They may seem to be positive or negative distractions; they may seem to be problems you face or pleasures you enjoy; but if they keep your thoughts away from the singular thought of God, they are distractions for you.

Do not feel guilty about your distractions, for distractions cause no loss in the Will of God. God's Will is truth, and so it remains always true. Distractions can have no affect on it. Distractions only distract you from what is true, so that your focus is on distractions, which distract you from the awareness of truth.

But then the awakened willingness within comes, and it calls you to turn away from distractions. It calls you to return your mind fully to the awareness of truth. In this calling, your distractions can serve the purpose of truth. For all things given to your willingness will be used by your willingness to further awaken the call within you. This will continue until your distractions are no more, and you are fully awake to the singular thought of God without distraction of any kind.

This is the purpose of John, the call within you that calls you to awaken. Follow the Voice. Listen to it. Do not let fear imprison this Voice within you.

It is as written in the book of the words of Isaiah the prophet:

"A voice of one calling in the desert,
'Prepare the way for the Lord,
make straight paths for him.
Every valley shall be filled in,
every mountain and hill made low.
The crooked roads shall become straight,
the rough ways smooth.
And all mankind will see God's salvation.'"

(Luke 3:4-6, New International Version)

📖(v 21 – 38) The most helpful way for you to view yourself is not to view yourself as special. The ego wants to see itself as special. Special is separate, so to surrender to the ego's desire is to continue to see yourself as separate from God. This is not helpful.

Do not look at Jesus' baptism and see him as special in comparison to you or others. Look at his baptism and realize Jesus was baptized with others and the same as others, in the same water and by the same one. For Jesus was baptized as one Son of God. It was of this *one Son* that it was spoken:

"You are my Son,
whom I love;
with you I am well pleased."

These are the words spoken *of you*. Read these
words. Listen to them. Take them into your heart. Accept
them as true of you as they were true of Jesus, for there
is no difference of any kind.

Rejoice that you are not special and that Jesus was
not special, for it is all the same. You are he, and he is
you. You are the one Son of God. This is your truth. You
are the Son of God, just as Jesus was. There is no
difference among you.

NTI Luke, Chapter 4

(v 1 – 13) Within your mind, there are confusing
thoughts that tell you that you are what you are not.
These thoughts are sly and deceitful, and you have
listened to them and believed them. You listen to them
and believe them to this day, so that they confuse you,
even to the point of confusing you regarding your
identity. But we are going to undo their confusion, for
there is also a Voice within you that is not confused. It is
this Voice you are beginning to hear and to trust. It is
quiet, barely audible to you at all, and yet you *feel* this
Voice within you, and you recognize it as true.

Together, we will follow this Voice into the desert
where the false voice may be exposed as false, and the
true Voice may be known as true. There will be great
rejoicing at this unmasking, for this will be the
realization of Self, which is eternal and eternally true.

(v 14 – 30) This is a course of looking within yourself,
for in truth there is nowhere else to look. As we follow
this course together, you will be tempted to look away
from yourself and look at someone else, but if you
remember that you cannot see anyone else *except*
through yourself, you will remember once again where
to focus your attention.

This is a course that looks inside the mind and
inside the heart by examining symbols that seem to be

outside. By looking through the mirror of your mind, we will discover the beliefs you hold onto there. We will look at your beliefs together and examine honestly what they say to you. Then you can decide if you want to listen to them or not.

Jesus came out of the desert a teacher, but the one who taught through him was the Holy Spirit. This is the same one that teaches you now, so that no time has elapsed since Jesus seemed to teach until the time that I am teaching you now.

And so, it is true of you now as it was true of him then:

> "The Spirit of the Lord is on me,
> because he has anointed me
> to preach good news to the poor.
> He has sent me to proclaim freedom
> for the prisoners
> and recovery of sight for the blind,
> to release the oppressed,
> to proclaim the year of the Lord's favor."
>
> *(Luke 4:18-19, New International Version)*

Today this scripture is fulfilled in your hearing. Forget not the purpose of this course. It is a course of looking within. This is the message of this scripture. This is the anointment you have accepted. Be grateful to yourself. This is the acceptance of peace.

And yet, even as your gratitude is being expressed, you will not have to look far to find doubt within your mind. There is doubt that the words I share could be for you. There is doubt that healing can occur. There is doubt that I am reality. There is doubt, angry and fearful doubt, within you.

Do not deny the doubt that you see. It is not to be denied. It is the part of the mind that rejects the healing that is offered to it. It will seem to resist the healing and to try and cast it away. But do not fear. In spite of its struggle and raucous noise, healing *cannot be rejected*. Through your willingness to be healed, healing will walk through the mob in your mind, passing it by in gentleness, leaving it in peace to quiet on its own.

This is the way we walk together. It is the way of peace and great joy.

(v 31 – 37) I am your leader in this process of healing. It is best for you to realize that you do not know the answers and you could not heal yourself. The way to healing is to listen to Me with the full attention of your ears. Focus them on nothing else and no one else. Quiet your mind, that you may hear only Me.

There is nothing within you that needs to be driven away, but it may seem that way to you. You may seem to be possessed of an evil voice that whispers torturous thoughts into your mind and will not go away. This "demon" is your fear. It will disguise itself in different forms in order to distract you from the truth of what *is*, but do not let it fool you. It is your fear of healing, so it must be sickness. For what else could fear healing but sickness? Does love need to fear healing? Does peace need to fear healing? That which is the effects of health need not fear healing, so it is your sickness that causes fear and pain within you.

Know your sickness for what it is. And remember that willingness is where you choose to give your power now. This is what you are to do when you see symptoms of sickness within your mind:

> *Acknowledge that you are sick.*
> *Remember you have decided to be healed.*
> *Turn away from the voice of sickness.*
> *Give all of your attention*
> *to your willingness to be healed.*
> *Trust in your willingness.*

It is your sickness that cries out, "What do you want with us? Have you come to destroy us?" And it is your willingness that answers, "Be quiet. We are listening to the Voice of Truth now."

(v 38 – 44) There will seem to be many sick thoughts within your mind that need healing. Do not fear that each one must be touched and healed for healing to come over you. For all sickness comes from the same source. When the source is healed, all of the symptoms of sickness disappear at once!

So this is what you are to do:

Do not believe the symptoms in your mind. Do not be distracted by them. Those small things are not the source of your sickness. But when you notice the symptoms, let them remind you that the source is within you still. Give your willingness to the Source of Healing, that the source of sickness may be taken away.

And this is what else you are to do:

Although there is sickness within you, you are not wholly sick, nor are you sickness itself. For your willingness is within you, and it is health. Turn your attention to your health. Live within your health. Be your health. Get up and walk with it, giving your attention to it, that it may grow within you.

Sickness must rest and be quiet. This is the way to health. Let your sickness rest.

But health must serve the Son of God, for that is its only purpose. Let your health serve in great joy, and be glad for it.

NTI Luke, Chapter 5

(v 1 – 11) Things are not as they seem. This is why I ask you to trust Me and follow Me. I know how things are. You are blind to these facts, for you only know what you think you know, and that is nothing but a deep and burdensome slumber.

Step away from what you know, and come with Me. I will show you what you don't know. I will show you what you don't think is possible and prove to you that it is true.

Leave what you know. Be willing to put it completely behind you, and follow Me. What you know limits you and holds you back through your own willingness to know it. Cast what you know away from you, and I will help you to pull in a net full of what you did not believe was possible.

(v 12 – 16) The journey that we take together will seem to take great faith. Do not worry that you do not have enough faith to complete the journey. For if you have faith to start, you have faith to complete it.

On this journey through this course that we will complete together, you will come to see yourself as dirty, unworthy and untouchable. All means of self-hatred will come up in you, but do not be alarmed. Your blemishes come to Me for healing. Your hatred comes to Me through your faith and willingness that it may be healed.

Hatred is nothing but a desire for Love that believes Love is absent. In My Light, it shall know Love is not absent. In this knowledge, it is healed.

Spend time with Me when hatred comes upon you. Retreat to a quiet place, and ask for My help. Wait in peace and confidence for My answer. I invite your unhealed spots into the Light that I may heal them. I will not abandon you when the unhealed spots answer my call and step forth to be healed.

(v 17 – 26) Again I tell you, you will find doubt in your mind. Even as I show you that you are worthy of love by loving you through My Self and into your heart, a thought will rise within your mind that says, "I am not worthy of this love. It is love that must be illusion, for I am an abomination."

This is yet another spot rising to the surface to be healed, so give this thought to Me. Let My Light shine upon it.

I am asking you to pick up your mat and walk. This is the task at hand. And to do this, you must be willing to leave your doubt behind. This is why I tell you that there will be doubt! So when you see it, you can say, "Ah, yes. There it is, just as I was told it would be." And you can remember that the Authority given faith is stronger than the authority presumed in doubt.

Lay your doubt aside. Trust in My words and walk with Me.

(v 27 – 32) Remember that you are sick, and I have come to heal. Remember all that I say, that healing may be ushered in now.

You are worthy.
Do not let doubt tell you that you are not.
Feel grateful for your willingness.
It will herald all healing for you.

Sickness must be seen to be healed, so show your sickness to Me. But do not forget that it is only sickness, and through your rest, I come to heal.

(v 33 – 39) Old habits must be let go, for old habits will not usher in a new day. With old habits, all things remain the same. But with new habits, all things are possible.

I have come to teach you new habits. You will learn these habits by practicing them as I ask. Remember Me, and practice.

You will catch yourself practicing the old habits, for this has been your way until now. Slipping into old habits does not ruin the new ones. So when you find yourself doing this, forgive yourself your attraction to the old by stepping away from the old and stepping into the new. Each time you do this, you help yourself to unlearn the old and to learn the new.

Take no old habits with you into the new, for the old habits must be left completely if the new habits are to result in new.

NTI Luke, Chapter 6

(v 1 - 11) Judgment is a way of looking at the world and deciding what is good and what is bad, or what is right and what is wrong. You have been taught within the world how to exercise your judgment so that it is "good judgment," for even judgment itself can be good or bad, right or wrong.

Now I ask that you forget everything you have been taught and everything you have learned. For if you know nothing, you cannot judge. Any judgment that you make and accept as a belief in your mind is a mistake, for any judgment that you make assumes something within illusion is real, and within its realness, something is better or more valuable than something else. Judgment accepts as real and then separates, so all judgment must be of the ego.

Look at Jesus and at the Pharisees within these scriptures. Surely you notice that the Pharisees have learned "rules" on which they feel they can judge. But the Pharisees are only a symbol of what is within your mind, for you also have learned "rules" on which you believe you can judge.

Did you judge the Pharisees as you read these stories? On what "rule" did you base that judgment? Is there a belief in your mind that Jesus is more "real" or more "truth" than the Pharisees? Did you think that the Pharisees were "wrong" to judge Jesus?

Nothing in the world is more "real" than anything else. This is *why* you know nothing and cannot judge. Your conscious experience is only of the world, and so you cannot know truth, which is not of the world.

This is why I have come to you. I know truth *and* I know the world that you believe and hold dear. I can lead you from the world to the truth if you will trust and follow Me.

To trust and follow Me, make no judgments along the way. Be as a little child, wide-eyed and curious, enjoying all that you seem to experience. Trust Me to make your judgments for you.

(v 12 – 16) Do not be bothered that the names of the apostles in one book of the New Testament do not match up with the names of the apostles in another book. These details are not important, because these details are meaningless. The apostles are but symbols, which represent everyone, and so there is no difference between one apostle and another, or between one man and you. We are all followers of the path that comes from within. We are all guided to learn the truth by following the path of unreality.

(v 17 – 26) The world is a great temptation for you, because the world was made as a distraction from truth. Everything in the world is not truth, and yet you want to make sense of it and make it real. To the degree that you can let go of the world and not be concerned about it, that is to the degree that you accept healing. And to the degree that you are involved in the world and taking care of its many problems, that is to the degree that you reject healing as the answer to its problems.

(v 27 – 36) It is within the world that you seem to be, so it is within the world that I come to lead you. But I ask you to look at the world differently now. No longer accept that there is a "you" and a "them" who is separate from you. This is the view the ego has of the world.

My view is that the world is all one song with different notes played in harmony to create the one. It is the song that is cherished, not the notes. And the song is being played perfectly by Me, who is the director of the music.

If you look at the song from My point of view, you see its beauty and perfection. But if you look at the song from the point of view of one note, who believes it is separate and competing with other notes, the song seems to be a war filled with attack and grievance and worry.

Remember that you are not the note. That is a distorted view of the music. *We are the song* as *one sound* together.

Love the entire song. Every aspect is equally important to the whole, every aspect valuable and cherished for its part in it. Share the perspective of the song by seeing yourself *as the song* and by loving the entire song, just as it is, without judgment or desire that the song should be played differently.

(v 37, 38) *Everything that you see and experience, you see and experience through the filter of your mind.*

There can be no exception. This is always true. This is why you can see or experience something in one way and have one opinion or belief about it, and another one can seem to see or experience it in another way and have another opinion or belief. All of this "seeing" is occurring through the ego-mind, which does not see at all. It interprets.

The ego-mind is itself a seeming split, apart from the Christ-mind, which is one. Since the ego-mind is a split or fraction, its perspective or viewpoint is not whole. Since it is not whole, it is not knowledge, which is why it interprets.

But the ego-mind is not aware that it interprets. It believes it knows. This is why ego minds seem to conflict. Each one merely interprets without knowledge, but mistakes its interpretation for knowledge.

Knowledge cannot conflict, for it is whole. Interpretation cannot conflict, since it is not knowledge. It can only seem to conflict, but that is a conflict of illusions or unreality, which is no conflict at all.

Everything you see and experience, you see and experience through the filter of your own mind. In order to find peace, one must abandon interpretation and remember knowledge. This is the process of learning that I lead you through. You are learning that you do not know; you interpret. This enables you to step back from conflict, and knowing that your interpretation is nothing, let your interpretation go. As interpretation is released, knowledge can be given. Knowledge is peace, since knowledge has no conflict, because it is whole and it is truth.

(v 39 – 42) Everything you see and experience, you see and experience through the filter of your own mind. This is good news, for what you see and experience witnesses to the interpretation that you believe is knowledge. Upon seeing it and knowing that it is not knowledge, because it is not peace, you can choose to step back and let your false interpretation go.

You may see your brother's error, which is his false interpretation that he mistakes for knowledge. I tell you that as long as you believe your interpretation, you do not have knowledge. Therefore, you cannot lead your brother to let go of his interpretation. For only knowledge can see clearly to lead mistakes to healing. Whatever you see in your brother, bring back to your interpretation, that you may give it up and be healed.

(v 43 – 45) You will speak from your interpretation as long as you believe your interpretation. So when you recognize that you have an interpretation, it would be wise not to speak. Do not fight for an interpretation that is meaningless, for meaninglessness brings you nothing.

When you notice that you have an interpretation, take a break from what you see. Seek quiet time with Me, and share your interpretation with Me. Do not share your interpretation as if you must be right, expecting Me to support you and lead you to the righteousness of your way. Share your interpretation *expecting that you are wrong*, because you have seen and believed without knowledge. In such humility, you can let go of your interpretation; you will see that it is nothing of value to you. And what you receive in its place you will extend, and that which you share shall be peace and restfulness.

(v 46 – 49) Why do you call me "Lord, Lord," and do not do what I say? I am Lord, because I am knowledge. To listen to Me and practice what I say is to find true peace that cannot be shaken, because it is knowledge.

But to listen and not practice is to keep your interpretation, which is not knowledge. And so you have chosen to keep nothing and believe it is something. This is to choose illusions over truth. And illusions cannot be shared.

Review My words and practice them. I am teaching you the way of peace.

NTI Luke, Chapter 7

📖(v 1 – 10) Listen to Me in trust and faith, for all that I share is important to your healing. You must practice what I share with you. You must remember My words and treasure them within your mind. Ask Me for more, and they will be given you. Have faith that you are worthy, and you will hear. For it is My Will that you hear My Voice.

When My Will meets your desire and the quietness of your mind, it shall be done, and you will hear.

This is what is symbolized in the story of the centurion whose servant was healed. He did not doubt that he was worthy to receive of Me. He did not doubt that his servant was worthy. The doubt that is written into the story was added by others who did not know their worth or the worth of others. But the centurion did know. And so, his desire and the quiet faith of his mind joined with the knowledge in Mine, and as one Will *without separation*, what was asked was given.

Ask for the healing of your mind by asking that My thoughts be placed there. As you seek, you shall find. You cannot fail to find that which you seek in honesty of faith.

(v 11 – 17) There is no death, but within you there is a deep slumber that resembles death, for it is unaware of truth or of Life. I have come to awaken you from this slumber and to resurrect you from this death. Yet each one is dead by his own choice, so each one must choose to answer My call to resurrection.

I am calling to you now. My hand is outstretched to assist you as you rise. What is your choice? Are you ready to awaken to Life?

(v 18 – 23) There are expectations in your mind regarding truth, but these expectations are based on what you know within your slumber. They are not based on knowledge or Life. They are based on interpretation, or death.

What do you expect of Me? Where is it that you think I am leading you to?

Free yourself from these thoughts, and open your mind to Me unfettered by expectations. Blessed is the man who does not fall away on account of Me.

(v 24 – 28) Why did you begin this search? What is it that you wanted to find? Did you really expect to find the peace of God in *your way*?

No, you expected surrender. This was the expectation given you by Me. That is why this expectation crossed your mind in peace with willingness.

This path that you have chosen is the greatest of all paths within the world. Yet, this path is *within the world*. To know the kingdom of Heaven, you must be willing to step off of this path with Me.

(v 29 – 35) In honesty, look at your expectations and at what you want. Were your expectations given to you by Me? If they were not, then they are not of Me, and you will not know Me if you judge Me by them.

(v 36 – 50) Your surrender *is* forgiveness. To the measure that you surrender to Me, that is the measure that your thoughts, which are not of Me, are forgiven. For when you are accepting My thoughts and doing My Will with recognition that they are your thoughts and your Will, you are not living as a separate entity. You are being one Will with Me. And this *is* forgiveness, which is where your love comes from. For you can only know love when you accept Love and join with the Will of Love. But to join with a will that is not Love is to choose to be separate from Love. That is to choose to remain asleep and to say "no" to the offer of resurrection, which is an offer extended to you *now*.

NTI Luke, Chapter 8

(v 1 – 15) You are looking at yourself now and seeing what you believe is your unworthiness. As you compare yourself to others, you note that you are not good enough. You do not give enough or practice enough. In your own judgment, you are never enough.

Let's review what I have asked of you. I have asked you to trust that you are worthy. I have asked you to let your sickness rest. I have promised that we would look at your sickness together, and I have asked you to nurse your willingness with gratitude.

Now is a time for gratitude and rest. Be grateful that you have been willing to bring your sickness to Me. Rest, as we look at your sickness together. For it cannot be healed if it is hidden from healing.

Focus on your gratitude. Let the guilt and hatred and anger rise. Remember that you are being healed, even now. Do not nurse your sickness. Let it come up, but choose to nurse your willingness to be healed.

Let all things serve the purpose of healing. Do not avoid healing because you do not want to look at the pain of sickness. We must look at it together if you are to be healed.

Do not be afraid. I am with you, even now. Stay with the process. Be the good soil that produces a crop.

(v 16 – 18) I have already told you that this is a course of looking within. And yet, your mind wanders to the world as the source of guilt. Nothing within the world is the source of guilt. Not even what you do within the world can be a source of guilt for you.

The outer is a reflection of the inner, because all that you see and experience, you see and experience through the filter of your mind. If you believe that you see or experience guilt, the judgment of guilt must already be in the mind. So a part of your healing process is to let loose the judgment you have already put upon yourself.

What comes first *is first*. But when what comes first is changed, all that follows must change also.

(v 19 – 21)   *There is only one Will,*
and that is God's Will.

(v 22 – 25) The storm that is raging is within your mind. It rages there because you are asleep. If you were awake to the Will of God, your one true Will, you could perceive no storm, for there is none. This is the lesson we will learn together. Trust in Me as your Teacher. I will show you that you are at peace.

(v 26 – 39) The storm that rages within your mind is like cloud cover, hiding the peacefulness behind it. But the peace is within you also. And peace is your natural state.

Our purpose is to blow away the clouds so that they disperse, and the naturalness that is within is what is left and is seen and is witnessed.

(v 40 – 56) There is a thought within your mind that says the healing that I speak of is impossible, and it cannot be accomplished. That is because there is also a thought in your mind that believes the cloud cover is all that you are, and it does not see how "all that you are" can be made perfect.

This is the thought that I have told you about. This is the thought that you are inherently unworthy. This is a thought that focuses on the cloud cover as all there is, and it does not realize that you are the infinite blue sky that rests behind the clouds. To realize your truth, you must have faith that the thought that you are the clouds is wrong. It is a mistaken thought.

Yet, it is a thought that you believe. In order to discover for yourself that this thought is totally false, you must be willing to look beyond the clouds with Me. You must be willing to take your eyes off of what you believe is true, and in faith, look with Me beyond that limit. To stop at the limit will not show you what is beyond it.

You do not know what is true, but you can take My hand in faith and walk with Me to what *I know*. In coming with Me and seeing beyond the clouds, you shall realize that truth has always been true, and peace has reigned unchallenged while you merely looked away for a little while.

NTI Luke, Chapter 9

(v 1 – 6) Everyone who reads My Word, listens to My Word and practices My Word *teaches* My Word. There can be no exception. You, who are reading this now, are My holy teacher.

Do not let this make you afraid. Do not worry about what is expected of you based on this "assignment." Nothing is expected of you except one thing: *That you listen to Me.*

Do not worry where you are to go, what you are to do, what you are to say or to whom. Do not worry how you are to teach. I may have you teach without a single spoken word.

Give no thought to the future. Give no thought to how you are to teach or when or where. Only give thought to listening to Me and practicing as I ask you to practice. In this way, you *do* teach, and the lesson you teach is heard throughout the world.

(v 7 – 9) There is fear in your mind. And so it will bring doubt that you do as I ask you to do. It will bring doubt that you are the one I ask to do these things. Do not listen to your doubt. It is to *you* that I am speaking. You who are reading these words, without exception for any reason, you are the one.

(v 10 – 17) You do not understand the power in your mind. That power is unspeakable in your world, for it cannot be described. But know this:

Every thought that you accept
teaches within the mind of man.

The single mind that you are is taught through the thoughts that you agree to think. And this is how you are to teach the world.

Although I may guide you to speak, it is not through your speaking that you teach. Although I may guide you to go or do, it is not through your going or doing that you teach. To speak to those or to go here or to do that would be to limit your teaching to a few. You, who are unlimited within your Self, cannot be limited by restrictions such as these. So it must *not* be through your speaking or your going or your doing that you teach.

Every thought that you think is heard *literally* around the world. The consciousness of man is shaken by your every thought. And so it is through thought that you teach, no matter what you are saying or doing, and no matter where you are.

And so I say to you again, dear teacher:

Listen to Me.
Remember My words,
and practice all that I say.

The fish that you eat feeds a multitude of men.

(v 18 – 27) You are the Christ, because the Christ of God is within you, and it is Christ that is your true Self. This is the health within. This is the Light that shines its healing rays throughout your mind, shining away all sickness in every form.

Peace be with you, my brother, for you are the blessed one. Put your faith with Me, focused upon your reality. It is this reality we seek to remember.

Do not be afraid of what must come before you are to remember. There is nothing that can hurt when your mind stays focused with Me. I am your constant companion, and I lead you through all things.

(v 28 – 36) A vision of Light is within your mind. To know this Light, you must only ask to remember it, for the Light is with you always. If you feel afraid or doubtful or desperate for love, all that you need do is quiet yourself and ask for Light. It cannot fail to appear within your mind at your request. It is always there to comfort you and to shelter you.

Do not turn away from the Light. Do not be afraid that you nag it with your requests. It is there *for you*, to serve you through your every moment of need.

(v 37 – 45) You will not be healed by following the ways that make sense to you. Following what makes sense to you has brought you to the point of needing healing, and so it cannot be healing itself.

To be healed of the thoughts that are foreign, but seem natural to your mind, you must put your healing in My hands. Give yourself over to Me. Let go of any resistance you feel towards this thought. Remember that the result of giving yourself to Me is your own healing. You will be returned to your Father, so rejoice! The time is now. Place yourself fully and completely in My hands.

(v 46 – 50) I have asked you to be a teacher of My Word, and I am grateful for your willingness to teach as I ask. And now you must listen to the secret of teaching:

A teacher is a student who practices all that he teaches, knowing fully that the message he shares is also for him. In this way, anyone may be a teacher of My Word, for anyone may choose to be the student, and the student *is* the teacher. For the Teacher comes through the student in order that the student may learn.

(v 51 - 56) Always remember that as the teacher, you are the student, so all things are given to you for your learning. In this way, see all things as an opportunity to learn and to practice, and be grateful for all things. There is nothing that will be placed in your path that is not a gift from Me. See it as your gift and you are blessed indeed.

(v 57 – 62) To be My teacher, you must let My Word be first in your mind in all things. This is a perspective you shall hold. Through holding this perspective in willingness and trust, you shall know what to do through Me.

NTI Luke, Chapter 10

(v 1 – 24) Give no thought to what you are to do in the next moment of time. When that moment of time comes, ask Me then what you are to do. I will answer you in that moment. For each moment brings with it its own opportunities for healing, but if you are thinking of another moment in this moment of time, you miss the opportunities that are given in the current moment. In this way, your healing will seem to take longer, because you are not using the time you have been given for the purposes of healing.

Think not for yourself. Remember that it is your thinking that has brought you to the point of needing healing. Relinquish your own thought, and trade it for My thought. Now is the opportunity to trade. Lay down your own thought *now*, and I will fill you up with My thought.

Go, filled with My thought, and do not question the thought that is given. When you are tempted to question and to once again find your own thought, remember the purpose of your journey. Joyously choose My thought again.

You will seem to have many temptations. You will seem to forget My thoughts completely for a time. Do not let that distress you. The thinking you do apart from Me cannot hurt you. It can only delay your healing for a little while. So when you find you have forgotten, shake off the past and the memory of your forgetfulness. Now is a new moment! You help yourself by choosing My thoughts again now.

There is never backward movement on this journey. You can only walk forward on the path to healing with Me. When you forget and seem to fail, you have not failed or slipped backwards. You have only stopped and stood in one place for a time. When you are ready to continue forward with Me again, I am waiting there beside you, ready to take your hand and go forward with you.

(v 25 – 37)   *To love God,*
to love yourself
and to love another
is all the same.

This is the one lesson I would have you learn. There is no difference among anyone or anything within your mind. It is all one within the Mind of God.

How would you learn this lesson? First, you must give up judgment. For when you judge, you separate and see differences. And in this "seeing," you cannot see that it is all the same.

Go within your mind and watch the process that you call "thinking" as it goes on there. What you will observe is that it is a constant process of dividing, judging, selecting and specifying. It is the calculation that defines separateness. It is everything except the acceptance of truth.

This is why I have asked you to lay down your own thoughts. But I understand that before you choose to do so, you must come to see that which you think has value as being truly valueless. And this *is* the case with your thoughts, for as long as you hold onto them and cherish them, you cannot see the truth that is before you now. They are like a veil that hides the Light of Heaven from your sight.

I ask this of you. Remember these famous words:

"Love the Lord your God with all your heart and with all your soul and with all your strength and with all your mind. Love your neighbor as yourself."

And then remember there is no division in this statement. It is all the same. It is all one Love.

See the thoughts in your mind that block this Love from your experience, and then willingly lay them aside. Each time you do, a prayer is sent to Heaven upon the wings of your willingness, asking that you may lay all judgment aside and see the truth of Heaven.

(v 38 – 42) As you listen to My words and practice what I say, resistance will come up in your mind telling you that doing all that I say is not rational or sensible. This thought will imply that you will somehow suffer or regret listening to Me. When this thought comes, remember that I told you it would. Then place it aside, and continue to listen to Me.

NTI Luke, Chapter 11

(v 1 – 13) How shall you pray?

Prayer is the unceasing act of thought. With every thought, you pray for everything or for nothing at all.

How, then, shall you think?

I have already asked you to think with Me by accepting My thoughts and laying your own thoughts aside. My thoughts are these: They are thoughts of forgiveness, love, acceptance, gratitude and rejoicing.

Whenever you are not listening to My thoughts, you will know, because you will not be at peace and you will not be happy. This is not a time to chastise yourself, for chastisement is not among the thoughts that I give. If you are tempted to chastise yourself for forgetting Me, you must again be listening to your own thoughts and praying for nothing. This is the time that you should ask for your daily bread. This is a time of forgiving your own thoughts by laying them aside and again opening your heart to Me.

Ask and it will be given you. Seek and you will find. Knock and the door will be opened to you. For everyone who asks receives, he who seeks finds, and to him who knocks, the door will be opened.

Your Father is the extension of Love. And His Love has been poured out upon you. It is His only gift. Anything that is not of the gift of our Father is of nothing, and so it is meaningless and it has no value. Lay that aside, and accept the gift given to you by our Father.

(v 14 – 28) Your mind is split. Within you there is great willingness to do all that I ask you to do. And within you there is a great resistance that guides you away from the practice I ask you to seek. Let us look at your resistance, that you may be aware of its ploys. Then you will be able to recognize it and to choose, not with your resistance, but with your willingness.

Your resistance will distract you away from Me. It will give you thoughts that seem to need to be thought, problems to think through and solve. It will give you things to do that must be done if you are to be seen as worthy by the outside world. It will throw confusion at you so that what once seemed clear when you heard My Word becomes muddled and unclear, so you are unsure what to do. It will ask questions, and you will seem to need to know the answers in order to put your trust in Me, and so you will go out in search of satisfactory answers when satisfactory answers cannot be found. It will offer you diversions that seem to bring great joy and pleasure into your life within the world. It will bring doubt into your mind, so that you will have a desire to find out what is true without giving of your trust.

What are you to do when tempted by your own resistance? Notice it for what it is. Do not let it disguise itself as something important. See it as resistance and call it by its name. Then give it to Me, backed by the strength of your willingness. Together, we will redirect your attention to the path you have set out on.

Blessed are those who hear My Word and heed it in willingness and joy.

(v 29 – 32) Your resistance is nothing more than your desire to keep things the same, to keep things as you see them now. And you desire this because you desire safety, and you think there is safety in the security you have made. And yet, you fear yourself and what you have made also.

You are safe, but you are not secure, for security knows no illusions of fear.

Let Me lead you to both safety and security, which is known through the knowledge of your safety. Safety comes from the guarantee of who you are.

(v 33 – 36) The knowledge of your safety takes away all images of fear. In knowing your Self, you can know no fear. This is the Light that shines from within to shine on everything you see, to shine away all imagined darkness and to show you only peace, love and joy. This Light you shall share with all the world through your natural love of Light.

(v 37 - 54) Resistance will sometimes seem to be the light, and so you must listen closely within your own mind, that you know where your instructions and desires come from. Resistance will sometimes be subtle, and so you must listen closely within your mind, so that you know where your instructions and desires come from. A useful question to ask whenever you are prompted to fill your time with anything is, "What is it for?"

When you ask, remember the purpose of time. It is for healing your mind. This is its only purpose. If you are using time for any other purpose, you are not using time at all.

Ask, "What is it for?" and listen honestly for your reply. Any answer other than the healing of your own mind is but a delay in your purpose of your healing. Anything that is not a part of your purpose is a part of nothing.

So if you ask, "What is it for?" and you find that you have given this time another purpose, then ask yourself, "What do I want?" When you answer this question with the answer of your heart, you find the means and willingness to change the purpose of the current time. And this change is but a correction, brought about by your Holy Spirit, which knows your purpose and knows what time is for.

NTI Luke, Chapter 12

(v 1 - 12) Now let's talk about the work you are to do. You are aware that there will be resistance, *great* resistance. Do not lose this awareness, and always be on guard. When resistance arises in your mind in any form, let it go immediately *in gratitude* as valueless.

The work you are to do is within the mind. It is a work of being aware, not of the world, but of your thoughts about the world.

Right now, you think you are focused on the world. You think you are focused on relationships, work, entertainment and rest, but I tell you that you are not focused on any of these things. You never have been.

Even your thought that you are focused on the world is an illusion within the mind.

What you are focused on, and have always been focused on, is thought. In every moment in your seeming interaction with the world, you are focused on thought. And because you see yourself as a separate entity within the world, you are focused on thoughts that seem to be generated within the private mind that belongs to you. Let's look very carefully at this process f which you are barely aware, and yet it defines everything that you think, believe and do.

Whenever you look at anything with the body's eyes, there are thoughts in your mind about that thing. If you look at a chair, for example, you may think that it is pretty, worn out, available, desired, not desired, clean, dirty, etc, etc. The thoughts that come into your mind seem automatic, without any awareness or evaluation on your part. You may make judgments about the chair based on your thoughts, and you may choose to sit there or not sit there based on your judgment. But you never look at, evaluate or question the thoughts you hold about the chair, and this is only a chair.

The process that you call thinking, of which you are mostly unaware, goes on within your mind regarding everything in your world. You make unevaluated judgments about the work you do, the relationships you have, the pastimes you choose and the person you think of as yourself. These unevaluated judgments define everything and everyone within your world. And they are allowed within your mind without your awareness, your questioning or your evaluation.

So this is the work that I ask you to do. I ask you to slow down your pace a bit. You may choose how you will slow it down. Pick a method that seems most comfortable to you now, but find a way to reduce the distractions in your life, so you can take the time to become aware of the thoughts that seem automatic in your mind. What are these thoughts? What are they saying to you? Why are you listening to them? Are they thoughts of love?

Do not worry what you will do with these thoughts as you evaluate them. I will be with you, present in your mind, as you undertake this work of looking and questioning. For now, it is simply useful to become aware of the thoughts you think *and are focused on* when you think you are focused on the world.

(v 13 – 21) You may ask why you should do this work, especially when there is resistance telling you that you have better things to do with your time. I tell you that until you have evaluated the thoughts that are within your mind, you are unaware of *why you do the things that you do.*

Without the awareness that comes from this evaluation, can you be sure that you are storing up the treasures that you want stored up? If your time is spent based on the judgments made by thoughts that are not truly valuable to you, whose treasure are you storing up? Is it truly yours?

But if you look at your thoughts, evaluate them, determine that they are valuable to you, and then make your life by following these thoughts...well...then you can be sure you are storing up treasures that have meaning.

So first look at your thoughts. Then, when you have become aware of the thoughts you have allowed there, we will evaluate your thoughts together according to what is truly valuable to you.

(v 22 – 34) Do not worry about your progress on this path that you travel to healing. To be on the path and aware of the path and thinking of the path is enough. Let Me tell you a secret that will make your journey along this path simpler and more joyful. The secret is this:

As you travel this path, you will only have two experiences. It may seem like many, but in truth, it is only two. One experience will speed you along your journey in joy. The other will delay your journey a little while. The secret to a simple and joyful journey is to learn to discern between these two experiences, and then always choose the joyful one.

I have spoken to you of both experiences before, so this is but a reminder for you. The only two experiences that you will know as we travel this path together are the

experience of your willingness and the experience of resistance. Everything that you think you experience is either one or the other.
So do not worry about your progress on this path. Do not judge your own thoughts or actions, for worry and judgment do not bring joy, and so they cannot be willingness.
Discern carefully, my friend. Recognize the thought within your mind. And at every opportunity, choose the strength of your willingness. Seek only for the kingdom and all things will be given you. Where your Heart is, your treasure is also.
(v 35 - 48) It will be helpful if you remember this:

God's Will is that you be perfectly happy in every moment of eternity.

That is simple. And so when you are not happy, you have made a choice that is not God's Will. When you are not happy, you have chosen with resistance. That is all. It is not a fight or a rebellion; it is merely resistance. It does not take you from God or separate you from Him; it merely resists your willingness to know Him.
So whenever you are not happy, it is because you are resisting accepting truth. To be happy again, all you need do is return your heart to your willingness. Your willingness sings of God's Will. And so give yourself to it in every hour to know happiness.
(v 49 – 53) Let Me tell you another secret:

The world cannot make you happy, and so the world must not be God's Will for you.

Do not worry about the world. Let the world take care of itself, and trust that all things are handled in a loving way. You, my friend, are to follow your own Heart. Set your feet on the path to healing, and let your mind stay with the joy that comes from your willingness. Give no thought to anything else, and you will make yourself truly helpful to all.

(v 54 - 59) And so my brothers, I say to you all: *Pay attention to how you are feeling.* When you are not feeling joy, you have chosen resistance. Do not worry about your mistake. It is not held against you. See it only as a wake-up call and a reminder to choose your joy and willingness again. In this way, you wake yourself up. In this way, you make the choice that sets you free.

NTI Luke, Chapter 13

(v 1 – 9) When you look at the world, remember that you are looking through the filter of your own mind. When you find yourself reacting to the world you see, remember that you are only reacting to the thoughts in your mind. This will provide for you the opportunity to *see* the thoughts that you think.

As you watch the world through the filter of your mind, you will think you see many things. Some will seem good, heart-warming, funny, happy and desirable. Others will seem frightening, horrible, wrong, disgusting and undesirable. And there will seem to be a sliding scale of good and bad and every thought that is in-between.

Now, remember again that *you are looking through the filter of your mind*, which means that the concepts of good and bad must be thought of there. Surely, you will see that these thoughts are yours, and you are the proud owner of the judgments you have made. Recognizing that you own your judgments is important, for if you are the owner, or *the believer* of what you think, then you can also decide to choose again and allow yourself to think differently.

At first you may not see why you should want to change some of the judgments you have made. So I ask this of you:

Remember that judgment is like a knife that looks at the Son of God and separates him. This means that as long as you hold onto your judgment as something that has value, you are blind to the beauty and value of the sight of the Son of God.

And now, with that thought in your mind, can you give your willingness to lay your judgments aside, whatever they may seem to be? If you can find but a bit of willingness to see the Son of God, and so not to judge, that is enough. And if each time you notice your judgments, you give your willingness in whatever measure it may seem to be, that is enough again.

I bless you with My gratitude *each time* you give Me but the smallest measure of your willingness, for each small measure is like fertilizer; it is useful to Me in the healing of your heart.

(v 10 – 17) Your confusion comes from the binding ways of your own thinking until now. It is your thoughts that have made you suffer. And so, if you would choose freedom, you must also choose freedom from your thoughts.

This is why I have come. I am here to teach you to lay down your thoughts, to loosen yourself from your bindings, and to straighten up and walk in joy and gratitude instead.

(v 18 – 21) How does one come to know the peace and joy of God? I tell you that it is not through the worry and effort of your old ways. Sit down, and relax with Me.

One comes to know the peace and joy of God by listening to Me, as a small child who is eager to learn listens to a parent. And then, just as that child does, by trying everything the parent asks it to try. But if you watch a child when it is learning something new, you will notice that the learning itself does not seem to come from the child's effort. The practice is but an expression of the child's willingness to learn. The learning itself seems to come upon the child like a miracle, and suddenly the small child can do what it could not do before.

This is how it is with you. Listen and practice as an expression of your willingness, but do not expect results from your listening and your practice. Expect results from the expression of your willingness.

(v 22 – 30) There are many distractions that come to keep your mind from Me. Remember that distractions are temptations put forth by your resistance, and resist the distraction instead. I have said before that it is not important what you do, but why you do it. This is an invitation to do all things for Me. If each distraction can become an opportunity to hear My Voice, you are doing well on the path to healing.

The door to the kingdom of Heaven is not narrow. The door is open to all, and all shall enter in their time. But to pass through the door, one must pass by distractions. You do well not to be delayed long on your way. Make Me your only purpose in all things.

(v 31 – 35) *Your willingness is everything.*

Through your willingness, see all things anew.

NTI Luke, Chapter 14

(v 1 – 6) Now is a very important time, for now is the only time that you can take any action that will make any difference. In spite of its tendency to plan, even the ego understands the truth of the moment *now*.

(v 7 – 11) Approach the current moment with humility, as if you do not know what the current moment is for. Approaching this moment with this attitude is only a demonstration of honesty, for you cannot know what is coming or what you should do or where you should go. By approaching this moment in honesty and humility, you open up to hear My guidance within this current moment.

(v 12 – 14) When you approach Me within the current moment and share your prayers, do not pray about the problems you perceive within the world expecting Me to provide answers to you. Instead, think about *your reactions* to the problems you have perceived. What thoughts did you notice in your mind? What judgments are you making?

Think of prayer as an opportunity to empty your mind of guilt, fear, distractions, resistance and judgment by bringing them to Me. Think of prayer as an opportunity to renew your willingness and revitalize your faith. Then when this has been done, and without specific expectations, ask Me what you are to do. You will be rewarded with the guidance that is perfect for your healing in that moment. But know that My reward is not given because you have prayed as I asked. Instead, because you have prayed as I asked, you have readied yourself to receive the reward that I have been waiting to give.

(v 15 - 24) God welcomes all into the banquet of Heaven. In fact, it can be no other way, for one will not find his way into the banquet unless he looks to his brothers and lets them show him the way.

This is what I mean by that: The Spirit of God is one, and admission into the banquet is the acceptance of this fact, for *the acceptance and the banquet are one.* There is no difference and no delay between them.

You see your brothers as separate from you and frequently in conflict with you. This is an illusion based on the judgments within your mind. Without the judgments that separate, there could be no separateness. So in the absence of judgment, there is only one.

Many of the judgments you make are judgments regarding your brothers. I ask you to look at these, and I ask that you look at these judgments with willingness to let the judgments go. In making this request, I offer you the invitation to the banquet. Will you be distracted by your belief in your judgments instead?

There will be fear and doubt and confusion about whether you should do what I have asked you to do. Look at what I ask you to do in this way: I hold out to you the invitation to the banquet. You may trust in your brothers' perfection and lay your judgments aside, and that will be to accept my invitation. Or you may be distracted by your judgments and choose to trust them instead. It is your choice.

(v 25 – 35) What I ask you to leave behind, if you are to enter the kingdom of Heaven, are your perceptions of others as separate from yourself. And these perceptions are upheld by the judgments you make of them.

When you look at anyone, or even think of anyone, your mind busies itself in making judgments. They may seem to be good or bad or favorable or unfavorable, but what each judgment has in common is that it splits the object-brother off from others, of whom a different judgment is made. The judgments you make about yourself split you off in the same way.

So if you are to walk with Me on this path to healing, I ask only that you be willing to lay your judgments aside. Lay them down now, and your burdens will be light. Let loose your judgments, as they hold no value for you. Come and walk with Me.

NTI Luke, Chapter 15

📖(v 1 – 10) The one who seems lost, for whom you are looking, is you. That one, who is you, seems lost in the crowd of illusion. Because you believe illusion, there is confusion about who you are. So let's talk about that now, that you may know who it is you are looking for as you look for the lost you.

I have already said that you see yourself as a separate identity. This you willingly acknowledge. But you acknowledge this as a fact, when it is not a fact. It is a perception.

The you that is lost is not lost in reality, but it is lost within the perception of yourself as separate. For you are not separate and never have been and never could be. It is only this truth that is lost to you.

I have told you before that the truth is always true. The truth is that within all of creation, there exists nothing that is separate or apart from creation in any way.

I do not mean that each thing you see is a part or an element of creation, yet somehow independent as well. I mean that *there is no independence*. Everything that exists is one.

When you look at the world or think of the world, you accept that everything that is not of your body is separate and apart from you. Your friends and family are separate; the furniture within your house is separate;

even the clothes that you are wearing on your body are seen as separate from you. I am saying *this is not true.* This perception is illusion, and this is why I say that you are lost to you.

And so, this course must be a course in finding you. Everything that is put forth in this course must be put forth to help you discover the truth of you. This is why there shall be rejoicing when the one that is lost is found; because the one that is lost is all that is, and when it is found, it is all that is needed.

📖(v 11 - 24) Let's look at the parable of the lost son, which seems to be a story of separate and independent beings, but cannot be, since there are no separate or independent beings in truth.

The father within the story is the same as Me. There is no difference between us. You are the one who seems to be the lost son. However, you cannot be the lost son in truth, since you are one with Me.

The journey that this son seems to have taken is a journey in the mind only. In other words, you have traveled away from Me in the *perception of yourself,* but this journey has occurred in perception only. We are not separate in any way.

Now you are becoming ready to wake up from this imagined journey that you have taken. I have come to meet you and help you return to the truth of yourself.

Here are some thoughts I ask you to practice giving acceptance to:

The Spirit of God is one.
Nothing exists that is outside of the Spirit of God.
I exist, and so I must be within the Spirit of God.
That which is within the Spirit of God
is the Spirit of God.
I and the Spirit of God are one.
All else is illusion.

As we move forward, I will help you to see and understand these thoughts more clearly. For now, I ask that you give willingness to accept them. I also ask that you remember whatever is true for you is true of everyone and everything you experience.

📖(v 25 - 32) The other son within the story represents resistance within your mind. It serves no purpose but to deny that you and the Father are one. Do not look to the resistance in this story. Stay with your willingness. Stay with your joy.

NTI Luke, Chapter 16

(v 1 - 15) There are many questions that will come into your mind as you follow this path with Me. You will often wonder what is right to do and what is wrong to do. And you will feel confusion and worry within your mind. Let Me remind you that confusion and worry are not of Me. They are resistance, so you may rejoice that you do not need to listen to them.

When confusion and worry are upon you, simply rest and let them pass. When you are feeling peaceful and joyous again, do whatever comes into your mind for you to do.

Let me address the concepts of right and wrong now, for these concepts lead to confusion. Do you not notice that right and wrong are judgments? Have I not asked you to lay aside judgment?

Do not worry that you will be wrong in something that you do. Remember, I have told you that you will only have two experiences on this path: willingness and resistance. Choose with willingness, and you will feel joyful and all things will be helpful. Choose with resistance, and you have only chosen delay.

It is true that you cannot serve two masters. In fact, you can only serve one. In your willingness, you serve truth. And because only the truth is true, that can be the only master. In resistance, you serve nothing. For anything that is not true is illusion.

Remember that you are never focused on the world, and you will not be confused. Always, in everything you seem to do, you are choosing among thoughts within your mind. Always, in every choice, you choose between willingness and resistance, joy and delay. Keep these simple thoughts in your mind and you will not know confusion. Keep these options clear within your mind and you will always know your guidance. Choose to follow guidance and you choose health, happiness and the path of truth.

(v 16 - 18) The law upon which you make judgments is written within your mind. And in this law, you have placed your faith until now.

Now you are awakening to a new way to perceive. But you feel guilty, because your perception still seems to cling to the old ways of judgment. Let me tell you that of yourself, you cannot stop judging by the law that has been believed within your mind. That is because *you chose to believe this law*, and so the law is your desire. In order to have the law erased from your mind, you must give your willingness that it be erased.

When you notice that you are making a judgment based on the law, you must rest within the mind and give your willingness again. Do not believe your own judgments, for that keeps you stuck within the law.

What is the law on which your judgments and old perceptions are based? It is the law of separateness. It is the law that says the Spirit of God is *not* one. Or it may allow a belief that the Spirit of God is one, but it perceives that spirit as separate from you and others. And since the law is separateness, it must also see differences that uphold the law. Judgment is the servant of this law, for judgment makes the law master and confirms the law within the mind. Belief and acceptance of this law gives judgment purpose, and judgment gives the law reality. Without judgment, the law cannot stand. Without the law, there are no differences on which to judge.

Give your willingness not to judge, and rest when the temptation is upon you. When you do this, you give willingness not to serve the law of separateness, which is also to give willingness to know the Spirit of God is one.

(v 19 - 31) The story of the rich man and Lazarus has no meaning as it is written. And yet, the story is filled with meaning and true purpose when one looks beyond its words with true perception.

When you look at this parable through the eyes of the old law, you see two separate men. Although you are given very little information, you see a man in need of compassion and a man who did not give it. You may then decide that the man who did not give compassion deserved eternal lack of compassion, which he received from God. Or you may determine that in the end, God showed the greatest lack of compassion of all. It isn't important what judgments you make. They are all based on the old law of separateness.

Now let me show you how this parable can be seen when viewed without the law:

The parable is a collection of thoughts, which are being tested within the mind for value. The thoughts are not separate from one another, for each thought has been planned in order to conduct the test thoroughly. There is the thought of more and the thought of less placed side-by-side as if they are separate. There is the thought of suffering; and the thought of right and wrong are tossed in to maintain the illusion of separateness. The story plays itself out as a test, and as the story plays itself out, the scales of pleasure and suffering seem to tip. But all of this story is thought.

As the story plays itself out, it seems to become more confusing and more complicated, and one forgets that the story is only thought within the mind, pure illusion without reality of any kind. As one makes judgments, the story becomes more meaningful. It seems to take on life; and the story continues and is reapplied as "meaning" when similar thoughts come together in the mind. And yet, the story was never anything but thought without power to affect apart from the mind of the thinker.

So what does this story say to you?

All perception is thought within the mind of the thinker. The thought has no meaning of itself, but it is given meaning by the thinker. If the thought seems to have effects, it is the thinker that gives that thought any effects it seems to have. In other words, there is no power outside of the power of the mind.

This is a fact that I would have you consider now. Remember all that I have been teaching as you consider the impact of what I am telling you now.

Everything you experience,
you experience through the filter of your mind.
You are never focused on the world;
you are always focused on thought.
The basis of all of your experience until now
has been the belief in the "law" of separateness.
The Spirit of God is one, and everything that exists,
exists within the Spirit of God.
The truth is always true.

And now, what does this story mean except that it can have no meaning? And if that is true of this story, can that which you experience have any meaning apart from the meaning that you give it?

NTI Luke, Chapter 17

(v 1 - 4) Everything you experience, you experience through the filter of your mind. You believe in the law of separateness, but the Spirit of God is one. You have given your willingness, that you may be healed. Whenever you think you are focused on the world, you are focused on thought. Judgment makes thought seem real and gives meaning to thought. There is no power outside the power of the mind.

Now let's talk about forgiveness. Based on the law of separateness, you may forgive other persons for what they have done to offend or hurt you. You may also choose not to forgive them and to hold onto a grievance. In order to do this, you must have made a judgment that separates you from your brother.

Based on God's law, the Spirit of God is one. There is no separate one that can offend or hurt you. There is only a collection of thoughts, which you hold within your mind. Of themselves, the thoughts have no meaning. But based on past learning, learned through judgment, the thoughts *seem* to have meaning. And so you feel offended or hurt based on what you *think* you know.

Can you see how your brother has done nothing? Can you see how all meaning that has seemed to result in hurt has come from the filter of your mind? And can you also see how all meaning that seems to be applied is applied because you believe that the meaning applied is real? Yet, this does not mean that the meaning is real or meaningful in any way. It only means that you believe it is, and so you react as if it is. In this way, you *continue to learn* the meaning that *you apply* to your thoughts.

So what is forgiveness? Forgiveness is simply an acknowledgment of the truth of how the offense or hurt has come about. It has not come from your brother. It has come from the meaning you have applied to thoughts within your mind. Without this meaning, you could not be hurt.

And then, forgiveness is taking this realization one step further by acknowledging you do not want to be hurt anymore. You acknowledge that the meaning that has hurt you is within the mind. You are the owner *or believer* in that meaning, and so you are also the one that can let go of any meaning you have applied. And when the meaning is let go, the offense or hurt must disappear also, for there is no longer a power to influence an effect. What was made has been undone. This is the process of forgiveness.

And now, if your brother seems to offend you seven times in a day, your brother need *not* repent. For your brother has done nothing to you. You may choose, all seven times, to look at the meaning you have believed within your mind and to choose to acknowledge that instead of meaning, you are looking at thoughts that have no meaning in and of themselves. In this, you find release. In this, you begin the process of discovering who, or *what*, you are.

(v 5, 6) I realize that it will sometimes seem to take great faith to see your thoughts as meaningless, for you have taught yourself that your thoughts have great meaning. In fact, you believe that your thoughts have purpose. And that purpose is to define and make sense of your world and to define and protect you. This is the hidden meaning you have given them. And this is why you must lay your thoughts aside. For if you have made sense and meaning out of the purely meaningless, you are living within a world of illusion and believing it. In order to discover what is true, you must lay illusion aside, for you cannot find truth by looking through a filter of illusion.

This will seem to take great faith at times, but faith is nothing more than an expression of willingness. Call on your willingness, and remember it is your strength.

(v 7 - 10) You, my brother, are not unworthy. Being one with Me, you are as worthy as I am. You simply do not know your Self, and so you are unaware of your worth.

But I am grateful for your willingness and your desire to be healed. I do celebrate every step you take on this path with Me. Listen to Me and give your faith, that you may learn who you are and celebrate your worth with Me.

(v 11 – 19) Gratitude is a great gift that lives within you, for true gratitude is the recognition of truth. It is an inherent appreciation for you and your freedom. Gratitude, as the remembrance of truth, nurses your willingness to full health. Do not hold back on gratitude. Take time to sit in quiet and know your gratitude. To know the fullness of your gratitude is to receive a glimpse of your truth, for your truth *is* gratitude and love.

(v 20 – 37) Now you are learning not to look for the kingdom of God in a time or as a place, for the kingdom of God *is within you*. The kingdom of God is your Self, in your natural state of truth and joy when your misperceptions of yourself have been healed.

I have told you that you have only traveled away from Me within your perception of yourself. This is not an analogy or a helpful thought. This is the truth. In your own perception, you see yourself as something other than I Am. And it is this misperception that keeps you from seeing the kingdom of God, which is *at hand within you now*.

When will your misperception be healed? This is a question that has no answer, for "when" is a matter of time and healing is not a matter of time. Healing is a matter of willingness.

Forget about time and the future. Focus on *now* and the thoughts that are in your mind *now*. Lay aside resistance *now*. Dismiss meaningless thoughts *now*. Focus on your willingness and nurture gratitude for being. This is the process that brings about the healing of misperception, and it is a process of *now*.

The kingdom of God is within you *now*. Do not let yourself be distracted away from it.

NTI Luke, Chapter 18

(v 1 – 8) Prayer is a practice that increases faith and willingness, for prayer is *an act of gratitude*. Whenever you pray, whatever you may be saying, you are also saying within your heart and beyond the words, "I believe that there is more than this which I experience as reality. I am willing to extend my faith and follow this path, that I may know the truth, which eludes me now."

Continue to pray, that your faith and willingness may be increased through your own desire to have it so.

(v 9 – 14) Listen not to your own voice, which tells you how right you are in all that you think. Remember that I have asked you to lay your thoughts aside. Here is why I make this request:

Now you have a definition of yourself that you believe. It includes preferences and judgments and all manner of concepts that tell you who you are. But these concepts do not tell you who you are. Each and every one of them tells you who you are *not*.

Remember I told you that you have only traveled away from Me in your perception of yourself. These concepts, which you believe define you, are the misperceptions that tell you that you are not Me. These concepts, which you think define you, serve the purpose of separating you from Me within your mind.

Remember, you have journeyed away from Me *within the mind only*. It is only your perception that tells you that you are separate from Me.

So if you are to discover the truth of who you are, you must be willing to lay your perceptions of yourself aside. You must be willing to stop believing that you know who you are. You must be willing to be open to discovering your truth. This is the humility I ask for. I ask you to admit that you could be wrong about your definition of yourself.

(v 15 – 17) And this is why it is written:
"Let the little children come to me, and do not hinder them, for the kingdom of God belongs to such as these."

Make yourself like little children, free of self-concepts that blind you to the simplicity of truth. Open your mind to Me, and I will show you *what* you are.

(v 18 – 30) When one begins to understand what is asked of him on this path to Heaven, one must become afraid. That is because you believe that you are the thoughts you think. You have taken them on as your identity. And so, when I ask you to lay your thoughts aside, and I seem to make no exceptions to this request, there must come a time that you become afraid. For there must come a time in which you think that I am asking you to trade yourself for the kingdom of God.

Rest assured that nothing could be further from the truth.

I will never ask of you something you are not willing to give. This is because you are the Son of God, and what you believe is yours *is yours*.

But there will also come a time when you will begin to realize that what you believe is yours is nothing and that it has only held the illusion of value. In this realization, you will begin to give willingness to see differently. Through your willingness, your sight will be changed. As you begin to recognize true value, you will let go of the valueless, because it is value that you seek.

So do not be afraid. Be willing, and give Me what you can. In your gratitude for what you gain through giving, you will be willing to give more.

(v 31 – 34) Your understanding of what I teach will seem to come to you a little at a time. That is because understanding is the gift of willingness. As more willingness is given, more understanding is received. With full willingness comes full understanding, and then fear will be no more.

(v 35 – 43) The symbolism of the story of the blind beggar who received sight is clear and easy to understand. The beggar had willingness. The crowd seemed to represent fear, since they were fearful for Jesus to see this blemish-of-a-man within their midst. But the beggar did not believe their fear, for his willingness was greater than their fear. So his voice was heard above the noise, and the gift of his willingness was sight. And so it shall be for you.

NTI Luke, Chapter 19

(v 1 – 10)1The world of form is a preoccupation for you, because you believe form has meaning. You make comparisons and judgments and decisions based on what you experience or witness within form. I tell you that the world of form has no meaning whatsoever. It is completely meaningless. Any meaning that you think it has was completely made up within your mind. And because it was made up, independent of God's meaning, it must be illusion and it cannot be shared.

The meaningless *is* illusion, for it is not shared. And what is not shared cannot exist within the Mind of God. This means that your meaninglessness, to which you have given meaning, does not have meaning within the Mind of God. And so this means that it cannot exist.

This is great news for you, if you will accept it. This is the truth that will set you free. For this means that all meaning that you have applied that determines sin and guilt and fear to be real is in reality *meaningless*. And so this also means that sin and guilt and fear are completely meaningless and do not exist in reality, for any meaning that seemed to make them real is only the meaning of illusion.

Within this thought, the past is completely obliterated, for all meaning that you thought it had, it had not. The sinners have not sinned, and there is no cause for guilt. And this is why Jesus can look at one who seems guilty and see guiltlessness. Because he does not apply meaning where there is none. This is why you can seem to be transformed in an instant of recognition. The realization that all that you thought had meaning is utterly meaningless brings freedom and meaning and peace to all that you see and experience.

📖(v 11 – 27) If the minas in this story represented willingness, then this story would be at least partially correct in its representation. For the one with the most willingness would receive the most *through his willingness to receive it.*

But this is not how this story was intended as it was written down. And so, this story is in error, as *willingness is all that is needed in order to receive.*

Let us look at the error that is captured within this story and learn from it by looking at it another way. Error is upside-down from the absence of error, so by flipping this story over and looking at it again, we will see everything helpful that is here that we cannot see when we look at it with error.

The minas are meant to represent works. So if we turn that upside-down, it must mean that one receives through *no works.* And what can that mean? It can only mean that receiving the knowledge that is the kingdom of God is an inheritance that is given you because of who you are without any expectations contingent upon the giving. In other words, the gift is yours to realize freely merely upon your choice to accept it by accepting yourself as one with it.

(v 28 – 44) This is why you cannot judge, and your judgment, when you make it, does not serve you. It is because the world is written upside-down. Everything that you see and perceive is the opposite of truth. If you see it, and judge it, and make it real for you, then what is real for you is the opposite of what is truth. And so, you have invested your belief in illusions.

This is the symbol represented by the story of Jesus riding on a donkey. For the world would not show a king in such a way! But through this ride, it is symbolized that what the world would tell you is not so. You must be willing to lay down what you think you know and sing praises to Heaven for what is given. You must be open to receive what you do not expect.

(v 45 – 48) This is a time when you must be alert to the thoughts that have made themselves at home within your mind. I tell you, these thoughts, which sing the praises of the world within the temple of your mind, do not belong there, because your mind is the temple of God.

Rest with Me now, that you may see the thoughts that you believe, and you may also see that since these thoughts are upside-down, the truth must be their opposite. And then remember that only the truth is true, so in reality, it can have no opposite. That must mean that the thoughts you think and believe can have no meaning in God. Their only meaning has been given by you to uphold your belief and investment in illusion.

When you see how your thoughts do not serve the truth of you, you must extend your willingness to look away from them as the meaninglessness that they are.

NTI Luke, Chapter 20

(v 1 - 8) The authority on which I teach you these things is the authority of God and the authority of you, for both are the same. Without your consent or willingness, I could teach you nothing.

You may see Me as God or as a messenger from God, but I have already told you that you are not different from Me. Indeed, we are the same. So whatever I am, you must also be.

📖(v 9 – 19) There is confusion in your mind regarding who or what you are, and so you must listen to Me for a time. But when the confusion has left your mind, you will realize that you have listened but to your Self, which you share with your brothers.

The vineyard in this story represents a mind that is shared among God and His creations. And yet, although this mind is shared, it is also gifted to God's creations for their use. One of God's sons has chosen to keep the "vineyard" for himself. He has decided not to share it with his brothers or his Father. The son who has made this choice feels guilty for his choice, and so he expects a battle such as the one described within this parable. But I tell you, there will not be a battle. For the gift of God is given in Love according to God's Will. The Father will not send servants to take the gift from you. But since you are ready to return the gift to its Self, He has sent Me to help you return to it.

What is the gift? What is this mind that I speak of, which is represented by a vineyard within this parable? It can be none other than your Self. *You* are the gift that God gave to you, and He gave you this gift complete.

But in an error of thought and misperception, you have taken this gift and made it into something it is not. This is what I meant when I said you have traveled from Me in your misperception of yourself. And this story also tells why you feel inherently unworthy as a seeming separate entity. It is because you believe that you have stolen yourself from God.

But do not forget that I have also told you that you are the same as Me, one with Me within the Spirit of God. And do not forget that I have told you that you are God's Son, in whom He is well pleased. And do not forget that I have said that I am one with our Father, and I have come to welcome you Home in celebration.

(v 20 – 26) What are you to do? I say to you, do not deny your experience in the world. It is an experience you have chosen, and it is your gift to yourself, just as your Father gave a gift to you. But choose to use your experience to remember your truth. You do this by choosing to listen to Me, for I am the Voice of your truth. I have come, not to take away from you, but to give you back your inheritance, the gift that was given by God.

(v 27 – 40) God is the God of the Living, and so there cannot be death. For God is in everything that does live, and if death could take a thing that lived, death could take God.

You do well to understand that you do not understand. You do well to accept what I say without trying to understand it. For to try to understand is to try to conquer the thought and take it under your control and under your rule. But a thought of God's cannot be conquered or controlled or ruled, for all of God's thoughts must be free. Accept the freedom of God's thoughts without giving into temptation to question or understand. In accepting this freedom by extending your trust and innocence, you accept your freedom and your innocence.

(v 41 – 47) The one who will know himself is the one who stops the effort of trying to define who he is and where his place is within the world. The one who will know himself may ask these questions, but he will be satisfied when the answer does not come. For it is through no definition that definition is given. It is through no place that place is found.

Listen to the Voice within and do as it asks without seeking fullness of picture, and it is fullness of Vision that you shall see.

NTI Luke, Chapter 21

(v 1 – 4) And so I tell you:

True reward comes only from full surrender to God.

There can be no other way! Partial surrender is not to let go of control. And to keep control is to keep the truth firmly hidden from your sight, for the truth is not control. The truth is complete and perfect love of freedom.

(v 5 – 38) It is time that we talk about fear. For I have said that fear can keep you from Me. This is true, and it could never be true.

It could never be true that anything could keep you from Me, because we are always one. That is what must be true, or we would not exist.

But it is also true that fear can keep you from Me in that fear can keep the peace and knowledge of what I Am from your awareness, and this is to keep the truth of what *you are* from your awareness too. We have spoken of the mind that must be shared, which you believe you have taken for yourself. This mind, you believe you have stolen from God. You must know that it is impossible to steal this mind from God, because this mind *is* God, and God cannot be stolen from Itself. So how is it that you think you have stolen it?

The mind that is God is what it is, and it cannot be changed. But you, as one with this mind, had a wish that it could be different. And then, within the freedom granted by being of mind, you began to make your wish fulfilled. There is nothing wrong with this exploration of thought in which you chose to engage, except for the error in which you believed that your thought could not live if it was shared. In this error, you developed your first misperception of yourself. For in this error, you created the belief that you could be separate from God. And then, you judged yourself for what you thought you did, and you found yourself guilty of disrupting the existence of the truth that is God.

"Disrupting" is an appropriate word here, because God, as best as it can be described, is *sharing the existence of Love.* By choosing that God be something different, you had to decide that different must be that it could not be shared, and *to not be shared* must be a "disruption" of that which is shared.

This seemed to be the creation of a private mind with private thoughts and its own private abilities. But since you saw this as a disruption that destroyed the essence of what God is, you saw this as a sin and judged yourself as guilty. And what could come of such judgment except fear?

Now, take a moment to accept all that I am telling you, even if you cannot understand it as yet. I am telling you this:

The Spirit of God is one.
Nothing exists that is not within the Spirit of God.

You exist, and so you must be within the Spirit of God.
That which is within the Spirit of God
is the Spirit of God.
Therefore, you cannot be separate from
the Spirit of God.

You have believed that you are separate from God, a separate entity with private thoughts that are not shared. And for these thoughts, of which you believe you are responsible, you have judged yourself as guilty. And yet, there must be something within you that does not believe these thoughts are private, because you also believe you will suffer for having these thoughts, which means you know they are shared. This seeming conflict is the basis of your belief in fear.

Let's look at this more slowly once again, for there is an inconsistency here that you must see and recognize if you are to let fear go. The inconsistency is this:

You believe, "I have made a private mind with private thoughts, which are mine alone, which must mean that I am guilty of disruption of the sharing of thought that is God. And yet, I believe that this error I have made is seen, because I know that thought cannot not be shared. And so I expect and fear punishment for all I believe I have done."

And there, within your own thought and belief, is the insane idea that maintains your fear and yet can never be. For if you were guilty of making a mind that disrupted the flow of the Mind of God, that mind would be private and it would not be shared. Therefore, God could not seek to punish you, because He would not be aware.

What is the truth of all your thoughts and all of your beliefs? The truth is that they are based on a premise, a premise of separation, which cannot be true. And since they are based on a premise that cannot be true, your thoughts in themselves cannot be true either, which means there is no guilt and there can be nothing to fear.

Why have I chosen now, at this point in the New Testament to tell you this? Because when you look on this, I want you to realize what it is that Jesus intended his apostles to know.

It is your fear that makes the world you fear seem real.

When you have seen that the source of all that you believe is thought...a misperception within the thought of the idea of a private mind...you will see that it is nothing. And in that instant, it will be gone.

NTI Luke, Chapter 22

(v 1 – 6) The thoughts within your mind can seem to take you in circles. You can seem to move from understanding to confusion at lightening speed, which makes you dizzy. Do not let this concern you. When this seems to happen within your mind, you are witnessing your own resistance struggling in a fight for survival. Remember that I have told you this is your fear of healing. Remember I have shown you that your fear of healing must be sickness. Be grateful that your sickness has come to the surface where it may be healed. Remember that the way in which you let sickness be healed is simply to rest in its presence.

Do not get caught up in the struggle to understand what cannot be understood. Remember I have told you that this is a ploy of resistance. Instead, rest. Give your faith and willingness to Me, that you may be healed through your decision to rest and trust.

(v 7 – 38) There are two voices in your mind. This, I have told you before. But this I say again, because it is of the utmost importance. Your mind is split. This is why you hear two voices.

One voice may be most easily identified as "your thoughts," while the other Voice, when you hear it, may seem to come from God. Do not be deceived by what seems to be the difference in these two voices. The one that seems closest to you is the voice that is furthest from your reality. And this is why you have been confused until now.

Remember all that I have taught you. Remember the story of the vineyard, for that story will be most helpful to you now. How is it that one who has stolen a vineyard would be likely to think? Would he not feel like a betrayer, and so feel guilty? Would he not expect some type of reprisal, and so fear attack? Would he not prepare for his own defense, and also defend himself whenever he sensed the possibility of attack?

These are the characteristics of the ego, which are the thoughts in your mind that are based on the belief that you have stolen your mind, or yourself, from God. If you observe your thoughts carefully, you will notice that these veins are inherent within their flow.

But I have already told you that it is impossible for you to have stolen yourself from God, for you are within God, and you are one with God. Therefore, this entire flow of thought, all of which seems to have meaning for you, is based upon one meaningless premise. What is based upon meaninglessness and built upon meaninglessness must also be meaningless. Any meaning it seems to have is only imagined, and what is imagined is not real.

This is why I have asked you to evaluate your thoughts. Listen to the thoughts in your mind, whether they seem to be thoughts about you, someone else or thoughts about your world. Are they not based on a belief in guilt that is based on a belief in separate wills, separate desires or separate behaviors? Do they not include thoughts of fear, worry or a sense of foreboding? And do you not take actions or have thoughts of defending and protecting yourself? All of this is meaningless because it is based on a false image of yourself and your world. It is based on the false belief that all that you experience is separate from the reality of God.

Now let's talk about the other Voice that you hear, the Voice that seems to come from God. The Voice may seem to come to you as a *knowing* or an intuition, but when you trust it and do as it asks, you recognize it as God. This Voice seems based on safety, an inherent and invulnerable safety. This Voice seems based on love. This

Voice you call God, because it seems to be everything that cradles and comforts and cares for you. And yet, recognition of the Voice came from within you, which means something within you *knows* this Voice and remembers the Voice and recognizes its familiarity. What is within you *is* within you, and therefore must be a part of you. If you are able to recognize the Voice for God when you hear it, then God *must be within you*. And if God is within you, *you cannot be separate from God*.

And so, this is what you are to do:

You know that you want the comfort and peace of God. And now you know that this comfort and peace comes from within. So what you must do is choose the comfort and peace of God by denying anything that you recognize as alien to that comfort and peace. For if it is not of God, it does not exist. It is merely sickness born of imagined meaning. Therefore, there is nothing to do with it except let it be healed.

Where you see a need to defend, rest and let that perception be healed. Where you see fear, rest and let that perception be healed. Where you see guilt, rest and let that perception be healed. Whenever you think you are not worthy of all of the glory of God, rest and let that perception be healed. As you rest, you will be healed.

Within the mind of health, you will receive guidance. Trust and follow your guidance. It comes but from your true Self, which is based on truth, not illusion.

(v 39 – 46) There will be times within your mind when there will seem to be great fear as you move forward by doing all that I ask you to do. Know this:

Great fear is nothing more than great resistance.
And so the means for overcoming great fear
is great willingness.
Great willingness comes from
remembering what you want.

This is the time for accepting that the world is not real. For if you have given belief that the world is real, then you must believe that your fear is real also, and you will not be able to cross the threshold at which you stand and want to cross. For to cross over into reality, you must have accepted the awareness that what you know now in this world is not the reality of God.

(v 47 – 53) The time that will come will usher you across its threshold, if you but let it. For in order to crossover into the awareness of truth, you must not resist the crossing over by reaching for this world. This world, you must let go, because it is not reality. And so, you must seek reality over illusion, and you must do it in peace and full willingness.

(v 54 – 62) Remember what I am telling you now, and remember what it is that you want. You are on a sacred path, a path that is lit by the Light of Heaven. But in the hour when it seems that it may be dark, it is because you are remembering the world. Let go of the world. It is meaningless, based on a false premise and built of illusions believed. You do not want it anymore!

Let go of the world. Reach only for the Light of Heaven. This Light will lift you up, and you will not know darkness anymore.

(v 63 – 71) One will accept what he is willing to accept. He cannot be asked to accept anymore, for he will not even hear the request that he accept it. This is why you must be attentive to your own mind. For you are accepting that which you are willing to accept, but you are not accepting all that you want to accept, because you are not yet fully willing.

Do not let this distress you. Be glad that an awareness of limits has been brought to your mind. Be glad that the one who places these limits and removes them is you. For in this there lies a statement of your freedom and your truth.

This is what you are to do:

Watch your mind for limits that you have placed on your readiness and your willingness. Be willing that these limits be exposed to you. When they are exposed, do not defend them or fall into the trap of believing them once again. Instead, notice the limitation that has been placed upon your mind, and say to it but this:

*"I have limited myself by my own
choosing through agreeing to believe
this thought. But this thought has no
meaning in reality. By keeping it within
my mind, by judging it in any manner,
I keep myself tied to illusions. All there
is to do is to release this thought and
open my mind to God. I am willing to
be open to what I cannot expect and
cannot judge, for that is the experience
of truth, and truth is my reality."*

NTI Luke, Chapter 23

📖(v 1 – 25) The story of the vineyard remains helpful
to you now. For if you remember the feelings of guilt, the
expectation of attack and the desire to defend, you will
understand the thinking of the chief priests and teachers
of the law as they sought to have Jesus crucified. Know
that this story is only a symbol of that which is in your
own mind. Jesus is the symbol of the Christ, your truth,
which must be in your mind. The chief priests and
teachers of the law symbolize your fear, which is also
within your mind.

Let us look at your fear for a moment. Recognize it
as your own. For what you own, you can let go of. This
examination is a time of celebration.

Here is what you fear: You fear the loss of self, just
as the tenants feared the loss of the vineyard. But loss of
self cannot be, because your true Self was given you by
God as a gift. This gift shall never be taken away.

So what is it that you fear really? You fear the loss of
an illusory self, because you have forgotten who you are.
You think that to lose who you think you are is to lose
who you really are, but as I have already told you,
nothing could be further from the truth.

If I am to help you release your fear, I must teach
you that there is nothing to fear. This is why I have given
you the symbol of Jesus. For he has stepped forth into
that which you fear most of all, and he has arisen in glory
and joy.

Fear not! You are the same as he, and he and I are one, just as you and I are one. There is no cause for fear or sadness. This is a time for celebration, for you are opening up to that which you *are*.

Look at Jesus, and know it is yourself you look upon. Behold! Your glory has become manifest in this symbol. Lay your other thoughts aside and do not listen unto them, for those voices have no meaning now. Your truth is before you, and it stands silent before the world.

(v 26 – 43) The Christ is the one within you that does not crucify the Son of God. This one is there, within you. Fear not that He is not.

To crucify is to want dead. This is the voice within that fears attack, and so it seeks salvation by attacking first. This is the voice of the ego. This is the voice that has arisen within your thoughts as a result of the belief that you have stolen yourself from God. This voice does not love; it fears. Even within its illusions of love, it fears, which is why it attacks the ones that you set out to love.

The voice of crucifixion cannot help but crucify, for that is what it was made to do. Do not hate this voice when you hear its shrieks of attack. Calmly forgive this confused and fearful voice.

"Father, forgive them, for they know not what they do."

Look beyond this voice to the beauty that lies within. Listen in rest for the Voice that does not crucify and knows no crucifixion. This is the Voice your Father gave to you. This is your true Voice, the gift of Heaven that cannot be taken away. This Voice knows no crucifixion, because it knows no purpose other than love, acceptance, joy and oneness. This Voice welcomes your brothers as one with it. This Voice welcomes you.

This is the Voice of Peace. It knows no conflict or attack. It seeks no guilt, and it gives the past no meaning born of artificial thought. This is the Voice for God. It is a mighty Voice that silences all other voices as meaningless and without purpose.

This Voice beckons to you in certainty and with authority:

"I tell you the truth, today you are with Me in paradise. Beyond the illusions, there is truth. Truth is peace, and peace is paradise, because it knows only truth and listens only to the Voice of Truth. Lay mistaken thoughts aside and listen to Me, and you lay crucifixion aside as purposeless and choose instead the purpose of realization of truth."

Jesus listened only to the Voice for Truth. He forgave his brothers their illusions, because he knew they were not truth. He welcomed his brothers in love as one with him in peace and safety, because he saw beyond illusions to the truth of Life, which is the gift of God.

You, my brother, are like Jesus. The Voice that is with him is with you also. It is the Voice of Truth that ends all illusions, and with it, all nightmares.

Trust the Voice of Truth. It is the Voice of health and of honesty.

Honesty is acceptance.
It does not fight or try to change.
It accepts in peace
that which is meaningless as meaningless,
because it is honest and does not wish for deception.

(v 44 – 49) Jesus' death was not significant, because of his last words:

"Father, into your hands I commit my spirit."

With these words, Jesus declared that his Self was not stolen from God, but was *of* God and was the same as God. This was the significance about what seemed to be his death. It was the declaration that *there is no death* that was significant and was heard by some who witnessed these things on this day.

What is the nature of God? The nature of God is Life. That which is created by God must have His nature, as it is His nature that is the element of creation.

This is what God has gifted to you and will not take away: Life. There is no threat that this gift can be taken from you. It is yours eternally. And you are *of* this gift, and you are the same as this gift, as you are *of* God and the same as God.

Confusion entered your mind when you believed that you took this gift from God. You believed that you made this gift according to your will, which was to steal it from God's Will. It is this thought upon which you judged yourself as guilty and unworthy, and so you became fearful and learned to attack.

But if you understand that the gift you were given is Life, you will understand that the gift has not been stolen, because it cannot be stolen. It is a gift that simply is.

When you surrender to this gift by ceasing to deny its reality, you surrender to Love. For what can the acceptance of eternal Life be, except eternal gratitude, which is Love?

This is what Jesus declared:

There is no death,
because the gift of God is Life.
There is no guilt,
because this one gift
that God has given cannot be taken away.

Death is an illusion. It may seem to be final, but it is not, because all that can be final is that which lasts when all else has ended, and that is truth and the recognition of the reality of Life.

(v 50 – 56) That which precedes the recognition of Life as it is, is rest. This is the true meaning of the Sabbath. The Sabbath is not a day set aside at the end of the week before another week of work begins. The Sabbath is a time set aside at the end of time, before the recognition of time as a set of limits ends.

The Sabbath is a time of rest in which you still experience the effects of time, but you no longer choose to participate in them. As thoughts come into your mind that are not the thoughts of peace, you rest from those thoughts and let them be healed. During the Sabbath, your healing occurs according to your own willingness to rest. As the mind is healed, peace comes over you, and you no longer fight to place meaning where there is none. You no longer struggle against the gift of God by choosing to divide it, define it and judge. You simply agree to be grateful for it and to accept it in its innocence and purity. The Sabbath is a time of rest and non-judgment. The Sabbath is a time of stillness and peace. The Sabbath is a time of giving your willingness, that it may be strengthened into full willingness and the full acceptance of Life.

NTI Luke, Chapter 24

(v 1 – 12) I have promised you that if you give Me your faith and willingness, listen to Me and do as I say, I will give to you an experience that you did not expect. This is important. It is important that you give Me all that is in your mind for healing, that it may be healed. What you do not give to Me cannot be healed, and what is not healed will block the experience that I give.

Search your mind for all of these things, and when you find them, give them to Me quickly without any attachment to the thoughts you have found. Search your mind for doubt, all manner of fear, hatred, anger, grievance, guilt, unworthiness, helplessness, loneliness, depression, striving, hope and longings.

Each thought that is not of peace and joy in the present moment can be given to Me. And each one can be healed in order to bring the unexpected recognition of Life into your mind.

Be like Peter. Put your doubts aside. Let not your fears hold you back from desiring the truth of Love beyond your seeming reason. Come and look with Me. Continue to trust Me and to seek that which I offer.

(v 13 – 35) The sickness that is in your mind is a sickness of belief based on a sickness of desire. This sickness is not sinful, but it is blinding. It is not sinful, because this sickness has done nothing. What has done nothing cannot be a sin. It has done nothing, because all that is true remains true, even until this moment. But the sickness is blinding, because it keeps you focused on itself through your own desire. As you focus on the sickness, you see only what sickness has taught you to see. This means that you do not see the truth, even though it is present and before you now. Bow your head and check your heart's desire. Do you wish to be deceived? Do you wish to see what you have wished to see, or do you wish to see the truth? When you no longer wish to see that which is not there, you shall see That Which Is. There is no delay between the desire to see it and the instant of sight. It shall be done in complete perfection in the moment that you want it above all that clutters your mind and your sight now.

(v 36 – 53) This is what you are to do: Remember all that I have taught. Practice what I have taught with your every breath. Do not be distracted. Remember that the truth is not what you see, so what you see must be mistaken. Do not believe it and judge it and react to it as if it is real. Remain distant in your interactions with the world, aware that you do not know, so that you may remain open to guidance from One who does.

Be grateful for all that is true. All that is true is this: Life, Love, sharing, extension and joy. These are the characteristics of God and of truth, of which you are one. All that you experience must be of these, or else it is illusion made up in the mind.

Do not believe that which isn't real. Have faith beyond the experience you know now, and another experience will be given in the instant that you have readied yourself for it.

You ready yourself in this way:

Listen to all that I have said.
Practice it with your every breath.

Do not move from your practice. Be clothed with power from on high in humility and gratitude. You are blessed within the being that you are this moment. Amen.

NTI Acts, Chapter 1

📖(v 1 – 11) The power of all truth is within you. The story
of Jesus is helpful to you as a guide, a tool, and a symbol,
but the answer for you lies not in his story. If it had, he
would have stayed on earth to provide the answer to you.
But Jesus left your realm and returned to the Father,
that you may be freed to find your answer within
yourself.

The Holy Spirit, which seemed to be given to the
apostles when Jesus ascended from the world, was not
passed on to them at this time. Only God can give the gift
of the Holy Spirit, and God has given this gift to
everyone. The gift has always been in the world, even
before Jesus. This gift has always guided you. But as long
as you continue to look outside of yourself for answers
and satisfaction, you are unaware of this gift.

When Jesus ascended and promised the baptism of
the Holy Spirit, he only pointed the apostles to seek
where the Holy Spirit already was. In this way, they
learned not to look outside for teaching and guidance,
but to clearly look within.

This is My lesson to you. I am here to help for a
time, but My purpose is to teach you to look and listen
within. For always, your guidance must come from there,
because always, the answer is there.

(v 12 – 26) The first step to listening within for the
guidance of the Holy Spirit is prayer. But to hear Him
truly, you must pray in a way that opens to Him. Prayer
is not a time of asking for what you want. Prayer is a
time of putting aside that which you want and opening to
any guidance that He would give. Prayer is a time of
gratitude for His love and wisdom. Prayer is a time of
surrender because you seek nothing less than His love,
wisdom and guidance for you.

Therefore, pray in this way:

Father, I do not know what is best
for me now, in this time and this place,

that I may be led back to You. Because I
cannot see the path I am ready to walk,
take my hand and send me your Voice
to guide me. I shall go where it asks me
to go, and I shall do as it asks me to do
in joy and peace and certainty.

The second step to listening for guidance is this:

You must trust.

You must not only trust the Voice and the guidance you receive; you must also trust yourself. For the guidance comes from you through your knowing that is beyond conscious choice. To doubt yourself is to doubt your guidance. So you must trust yourself and trust what comes.

NTI Acts, Chapter 2

(v 1 – 13) The Holy Spirit knows the way. The Holy Spirit sees the whole plan, not only your part in it. Therefore, you must trust all that the Holy Spirit asks you to do, even if what is asked does not seem to be for you. For the Holy Spirit does not look at the world and see separated sons of God, each in need of separate plans of salvation. The Holy Spirit sees one Son and one plan. And so, what He gives to you is not for you alone. To learn this is so, you must do as He asks and trust Him.

(v 14 – 21) The paths given may seem to be individualized and the experiences may seem personal, but I assure you that they are not. Everything that is given by the Holy Spirit is given for all and to all, as the Holy Spirit does not see separate parts, but only one. When you hear stories of your brother's and your sister's experience with the Holy Spirit, rejoice and know that experience was also given for you. In this way, you demonstrate trust. Through the demonstration of trust, trust shall grow within you, that you may hear and see more.

(v 22 – 35) There will be symbols and there will be symbols of symbols, but always it is true that only the truth is true. Therefore, do not be caught up in your symbols. Do not identify with them, fight for them or argue with your brother about the symbols you choose to love. In this way, the symbol becomes but another idol that blinds you to the truth. Remember that Jesus left the earth so you would not make an idol of him, but that you would learn from him the way of truth.

(v 36) Therefore, know and remember this, because this is what Jesus taught:

There is no death,
and the answer that you seek
is already here within you.

(v 37 – 41) Peter was a teacher, but when he spoke, the Holy Spirit spoke through him. And when the people listened, the Holy Spirit listened for them, pointing to the words they were to hear.

Do not be confused by all that you see and hear and experience within the world. It does not need to take a specific form to be used by the Holy Spirit for your teaching and your guidance. Since He is the overseer of all things, all things can be used by Him for your benefit.

I will teach you how to listen to Him in all situations and at all times. Listen to Me, and be glad!

(v 42 – 47) Your joy shall increase as you listen to the Voice of the Holy Spirit, for He shall lead you to see no value where there is none and to know the love that is already within your Heart. This love, which is the source of all joy, is not a special love that includes some, but not all. It is an encompassing love, from which joy comes bursting forth from your Heart into the world that you see.

NTI Acts, Chapter 3

(v 1 – 10) Peter was a teacher who gave what he had, and what he gave came to him from the Holy Spirit.

It was through giving it that Peter learned he had it to give, for he could not give it if it was not already his.

The miracles that Peter witnessed, he witnessed for himself within his own mind. And these miracles were extended to others, that they too may begin to learn who they are. This is what made Peter a great teacher. He shared all that he had, recognizing that it was for all. And through this practice, Peter came to see that all were not separate, but they were one.

(v 11 – 26) The ego is the thought within the mind that separates. The ego says that what is true is not true, and what is not, is the truth. But the ego is not the truth, and so its words cannot be believed.

You experience the ego as a stream of thoughts within the mind that seem to interpret, counsel, identify, judge and spring forth as ideas. In themselves, these thoughts seem to be nothing to you, although you listen to them and act on all that they say. These thoughts rule your mind and your interpretation of the world, because you believe what they say. Yet, they are based on a foundation of separateness, which is not what is true. And so what is true is not in what they say.

To listen to these thoughts and believe them is ignorance, for you are listening to what is not true, but believing what you hear. Any action you take based on these thoughts is ignorant action, for it is action based on untruth in an unreal world.

Ignorance is not guilt. It is a call for knowledge. It is the Holy Spirit that leads you through corrected perception to the right-knowledge that you seek. Right-knowledge is true knowledge, and true knowledge is the knowledge of truth.

Do not worry about the mistakes you have made. They are based on ignorance, which is illusion and affects only that which is not reality. Be happy that you have been mistaken! Be joyous that there is another way to see! This is what it means to repent. To repent is to choose again. To repent is to decide to turn from the ways of ignorance and turn to the Voice of Knowledge. This is a joyous decision, for this is the decision that changes all things. This decision that you have made is a decision to listen to another Voice. It is the decision to let go of the thoughts you have listened to until now and to listen to another Voice, the one that comes from God. This decision is a decision to change the habits you have had until now. It is a decision to see yourself through new eyes, eyes that are based on a foundation of truth. This is why I am here. I am here to help you make this change from believing in the false to listening to the Voice of what is true. This is the decision of your joy. This is your path. This is your way. And I will help you, until you do not need this help anymore.

NTI Acts, Chapter 4

📖(v 1 – 22) I have told you before that you will be tempted to deny your guidance. And I have told you where this temptation will come from. It is resistance born of a sense of unworthiness. I have also told you where this sense of unworthiness comes from. It is born of guilt, born of the belief that you have stolen yourself from God.

Here lies another contradiction that you must look at slowly and carefully:

You believe you have stolen yourself from God. That is to say, you believe you have made yourself separate from God's Will. You believe it is your choice to follow God's Will *or* your own, and you feel guilty for this choice, because you believe it is a sin to have made a will that is separate from God's.

Your guilt, born of the choice to have a separate will, leaves you feeling unworthy of God's Will. And so, out of your guilt and sense of unworthiness, you deny God's Will by not hearing it, or by hearing it, but by not believing you are deserving to follow it.

There are several things you must look at here. First, you *do* have the desire to know and follow God's Will. Hold that up as a beacon. That is your willingness. Let it guide you to your true Heart's desire.

Secondly, the feeling that seems to be an obstacle to knowing and following God's Will is the belief that you are unworthy of God's Will. This is like a crafty trick. It is a loop that keeps you trapped within an illusion of yourself.

You think you are guilty because you
want to serve a will other than God's,

and

Your true desire is to serve God's Will,
but your sense of unworthiness is an
obstacle to that desire.

Do you see the loop in which you are snared? Can you see how your own belief in your guilt and unworthiness seems to lead you onto the path of increased guilt and additional unworthiness?

This is why I have come, to help you look at the upside-down reasoning within the mind that keeps you feeling trapped. And also to help you see that you are *not trapped*, because you can lay down this reasoning that makes no sense. When you lay it down and put it aside, you are free to know the reasoning of the Holy Spirit, which is right-reasoning and is joy.

Remember this story of Peter and John as a symbol to help you hold onto your willingness. Know that as they listened to pleas to lay down their purpose, there were doubts in their minds that seemed to echo the reasoning of the pleas. They were simple men, and they seemed to be taking on the history of the world with the new message that they taught. But know also that they did not listen to their doubts, their fears or their own sense of unworthiness. They trusted their message as the message of the Holy Spirit and the one Will of God. In following this trust, they gave themselves permission to do God's Will, which was their Heart's only true desire.

Remember this symbol. You *are* worthy of God's Will for you. You are worthy of the Voice for God and all that it will share with you. When doubt enters your mind, born of unworthiness and guilt, lay it aside. It is the loop you do not want. It is the loop that hides the truth from you.

(v 23 – 31) I have also told you not to be confused by what you hear, see and experience within the world. Everything is applicable to the purpose the Holy Spirit has set forth. Everything can be used for the salvation of God's one Holy Son. When the form of what you see or hear or experience confuses you, remember to pray to Me. Remember that what you look upon confuses you only because you believe in separate wills. If you knew that there was only one Will, you could not be confused.

Remember also that whenever you look at the world with the ego's upside-down reasoning, you cannot see clearly. Be willing to deny what you see, and trust that there must be another way to understand the situation you look upon.

Pray, then, in this way:

> *Oh Father, I come to you now in*
> *humility and gratitude. I am humble,*
> *because I realize that I do not know*
> *how to see. I cannot see the Holy Spirit's*
> *plan, and so I do not know what I look*
> *upon. But I also come in gratitude,*
> *because I trust that the Holy Spirit does*
> *know, and the plan is safe with Him as*
> *the overseer of all things. Amen.*

Then give yourself to your Father's Will, offering that you may be used for the purpose of healing, without the desire to judge. This is to lay yourself aside and to do your part in your Father's plan. This is God's Will for you. This is how you can be useful to the whole.

(v 32 – 37) To give of yourself is to give as you are asked to give without judgment. Whenever you notice guilt within your mind, you have judged, and so you are not listening with full desire to only be useful. You are also asking that you may decide what is right and what is wrong, which means that you are asking that you may exercise a will of your own.

Do not let this realization upset you. Indeed, you may laugh when you find it within yourself. It is nothing more than another ploy of the desire to hide your true desire from you. It is another loop that leads you nowhere. It is another opportunity to remind yourself that you do not know the plan, and therefore, you cannot judge.

Be happy. You are only asked to do what you are asked to do. If you do all that you are asked, you have done enough. There is nothing more to give, having given everything that you have been asked to give.

Give in joy, knowing it is your true Will to give. Let go of guilt, knowing it is just the illusion of an illusory will. For any will that seems separate from God's Will must be an illusion, for you *do know* that your true Will is always the same as His.

NTI Acts, Chapter 5

📖(v 1 – 11) This story is symbolic and is not to be taken literally. This story is a picture of the guilt that you have claimed and projected onto the world. This story has no meaning, except that it is untrue. And it is important that you see it as untrue *for you* also.

An obstacle to hearing the Holy Spirit is your own sense of guilt and unworthiness. This story demonstrates just how guilty you believe you are. Notice that Ananias and his wife dropped dead from their guilt. Imagine the magnitude of the guilt that seemed to be within them. But what crime did this couple commit? They sold land that belonged to them and gave a portion of the money that they made to the apostles of their own free will. Could this be called a crime? Even within your world, this could not be called a crime. To give in this way is generosity. So, what was their crime?

This story seems to say that the crime this couple committed is the crime of not being honest with God; it is the crime of hiding something from God; it is the crime of keeping something for yourself. It is *this* we must look at, because it is this you think you have done.

It is this for which you feel guilty, and it is this guilt that seems to bring on your death. We will talk about this guilt slowly and carefully, that you may look at this belief deeply and with right-reason, so you may choose to release a belief that you do not need to keep.

First, we must discuss what God is. I have told you that God is Life, and that Life is eternal. Since you accept that God is eternal and God gives life, this may not be difficult for you to accept. So let's take this thought another step.

God is Life, and you live,
so Life must be within you.

This means that God is within you also.

At this point, you may feel a temptation to pull away from My logic, but please do not pull away just yet. Let's examine why you want to pull away and look at that closely.

God is within you. This is a thought that you are tempted to reject. The reason you want to reject this thought is because you believe that God is good, but you are guilty. Therefore, you determine that God cannot be in you, and you must be separate from God. If God is Life, which you have accepted, and you are separate from God, then it must be that you are separate from Life. And that is death. That is why death seems to rule your world. It is because you believe that your guilt keeps you separate from God.

But can you not see that this is another loop of reasoning that does not make sense? For right now, you *do* live. Right now, as you sit reading this, you live. So right now, you cannot be separate from God. Right now, God is in you and you are in God. There is no separation. Right now, your oneness with God is complete, and there is nothing that is hidden or not in accordance with your oneness. Right now, everything is perfect, because everything *is* God.

(v 12 – 16) What is it that you must do? You must release your guilt. There is no reason to hide it, for there is no judge to hide it from. God is Life, and He has given His gift to you. And you are living it. No crime has been committed, because you live. It is only the *belief* that you have committed a crime that must be healed. This belief is healed by bringing your guilt into the Light and finding that you are not judged. Released into the Light, there is no guilt, for God has witnessed no crime.

(v 17 – 20) All things written within the New Testament are symbolic. All things written there are for your benefit and for your learning. Give Me your willingness, that you may truly learn what I have come to teach.

You are not guilty. You are a child of Light. I have come to set you free, that you may sing of your innocence before your brothers. For your innocence is their innocence also. And in your innocence, they will find theirs.

(v 21 – 24) When your brothers look for you within the prison they believe they have put you in, they will find that you are not there. They will look into your eyes and find no accusation or judgment against them. In you, they will find their innocence. Through you, they too shall be set free.

(v 25 – 42) This is how you are to know your own innocence, for you must accept your innocence to accept your brothers', and you must accept their innocence to teach it to them. To know your own innocence, you must do this:

You must trust Me.

Even before your innocence is an experience that you realize, you must trust Me that it is so. For if you do not trust Me, you will not let your guilt come out from its hiding place so that I may show you it is false. If your guilt does not come out from hiding, you will continue to believe it, and you will remain in prison.

And so I am asking you to trust Me above the voice that says you are guilty. There are two voices you may listen to. I am asking that you listen to Me. If you listen to Me and step out into the Light, I will speak for you. Through what I say and what I show you, you will come to see that you are innocent.

So my first request is only this, and this is all that I ask you to do:

Trust in Me.
Listen to My Voice.
Let Me teach you that your innocence is your truth.

NTI Acts, Chapter 6

(v 1 – 7) Trust is the answer to the questions upon your faith. As you move forward with Me and do all that I ask, you will hear questions within your mind. The questions will come from your own temptation to judge for yourself, which is your desire to exercise your own will, which is the ego. But this is no reason to deny your questions. For the temptation to deny your questions also comes from the ego who tells you that you are guilty for questioning and that for your questions, you will be judged.

I tell you that you are not guilty *for anything.* I will hear your questions and answer them. Bring them to Me in joy and trust, knowing they will be answered. The answer you are given will point you in the direction of all truth, which is Love.

Do not fear Me. I am your answer. I will not judge you because you do not know. I will fill the gaps in your knowledge with all that you seek to know and have answered.

(v 8 – 15) Within your own mind, you will find conflict and attack upon yourself. This is because your mind is split. You have decided to let yourself be healed, but a part of your mind is not yet willing for that to happen. Do not let this concern you. Do not let yourself get caught up with the battle within the mind. For any battle is a distraction from the Holy Spirit and from healing. Let the battle continue within your mind and without you. Watch it peacefully, knowing that a battle that is not given all of your power and faith cannot last, for only that to which you give your power is true and meaningful for you.

NTI Acts, Chapter 7

(v 1 – 8) To trust in Me is to give everything over to Me. To not trust in Me is to want to do things your way. And this you are free to do with My blessing. But to do things your way is to continue to stumble. To trust in Me is to learn and remember your joy.

I ask for trust, because I reveal things to you one step at a time. I reveal things to you one step at a time, because you have lessons to learn with each step. If I revealed the entire plan you would want to advance to the end, and you would miss the lessons that are necessary to getting there.

Relax and give Me your trust. Know that the end is joy. Anticipate the middle as a glorious adventure with joys and surprises of its own. The path can be easy if you give Me your trust quickly and fully each step of the way. It can seem difficult if you choose to fight Me. (Ha. Ha.) But know this. I am not fighting you, My child. I am holding you lovingly in My arms as you struggle with yourself. When you tire of struggling, I am there with you, ready to proceed.

(v 9 – 16) The path that you walk with Me will have steps that are necessary to your learning. You may not understand each step as it seems to come upon you, but do not let the steps confuse you. If you become lost in your confusion, trying to solve things on your own, you are not learning your lesson and you cannot advance on the path.

Although the form of each lesson may seem to change, the lesson is always the same:

Let go of any fear that would guide
you to take matters in your own hands.
Lay aside the illusory will that you do
not want. Trust in your worth and in

Me, and ask for My Will. For in My
Will, you will recognize your Will.

Through these lessons, the merging of what seems
separate will occur into what clearly is, and has always
been, one.

Although you may wish that one lesson would
suffice in order to accomplish the inevitable fully, it will
probably take more, and it will most likely take many.
This is because your mind is split and not fully ready to
learn this lesson as yet. And so each lesson is a stepping
stone to the final lesson, the lesson that will end all
lessons. Enjoy your journey by realizing its purpose and
by celebrating the progress that is made.

(v 17 - 43) During this time of learning, there will
seem to be a battle in your mind. For when the battle has
ended, the time for learning has ended too. The battle
will seem to be a battle between two wills, a will that will
at first seem to be yours and a Will that may seem
unknown to you. At first, you may not even know what it
is that you battle, but you know you are following your
own thoughts and the result is confusion and discontent.
What you have not realized is that you battle joy by
thinking in your own way, and by laying down your own
way, you find that joy awaits you.

Along the path to joy, there comes a time that you
seem no longer fully dedicated to your own way. This is
because the desire for joy is calling you, and you begin to
recognize your willingness to lay down your own will,
which is also to lay down the battle.

You will have a time of seeking, asking questions,
learning and letting things go. And then the answers will
begin to be clear. This is a time of great celebration, for
you have found your service, and you are willing to
follow it. Yet learning has not been accomplished. For
the mind remains split, and the mind that is split will
continue to cling to its idols and fight for its own way.

(v 44 – 53) Be aware of the hatred and anger that is
within you, but be not afraid of it. There is a resistance
within your mind that will seem to fight your every

move. But if you remember this, it will make your journey much easier for you:

> *This resistance within the mind that first comes up strong is actually weak. Any strength it seems to have is an ancient strength, given to it a long time ago. It can use its strength to seem ferocious in the short term, but it needs your strength to remain ferocious longer. So when you see it, remember not to give it your strength. Through your remembrance, its ferociousness must die. And only peace will remain in its wake. And then, the wake shall die too.*

(v 54 – 60) Remember that all things are well in My Sight. I am the Holy Spirit, the overseer of all things. I see to it that all things are good, and so they are. In what seems to be your times of trial and tribulation, cling tightly to Me and do not let go. I will carry you through to your time of peace and celebration. From there, you shall be carried to your joy. This is a promise that I make, and it is a promise you need not fear. For it is the promise of your Holy Spirit, who's Will is the same as yours.

NTI Acts, Chapter 8

(v 1 – 3) Jesus asked you to rejoice when you are persecuted on account of him. This is what he meant by that:

I have told you that there is a battle raging within your mind. This is a one-sided battle in which you *seem* to fight against yourself, but you fight no one. Within you, there is a storm of rage and anger and hurt and fear and guilt, and it is the brewing of this storm that seems to be a battle. But it is not a battle. It is only a storm. And it is a storm with limited power built-up within itself. So when this storm plays itself out and is given no more power, it must die, and peace and light shall reign within you.

This is what Jesus meant when he said that you are to rejoice when you are persecuted on account of him: As this storm rises within you, do not fear it. Fear gives power to the storm. Do not feel guilty for it. Guilt is the fodder of the storm itself. Instead, rejoice!, knowing that the storm cannot last, and that which comes after it is peace.

(v 4 – 8) Remember your purpose in all things. As the storm seems to rage within, there is also willingness. Cling to your willingness as a beacon of Light. Let its miracles protect you from the storm. Rest within its Light, and let its Light heal you.

📖(v 9 – 25) The process of learning seems to be a stepped process in which one man listens and learns, and then he teaches another so that he listens and learns too. This is how it seems to be. This is how it seems to be to you. But to the Holy Spirit, another thing is happening.

I have told you that there is one Son of God, and I have told you that the Holy Spirit has one plan for one Son of God. This is how the Holy Spirit sees. He sees one. And this is what the Holy Spirit knows. There is one mind in need of awakening. So this is how the Holy Spirit works. He works through you to awaken one mind unto itself.

When the Holy Spirit looks at the world, it does not see holy men and men of darkness. It does not see men at all. It does not see men who are right in what they do and men who are wrong. It does not see men at all.

It is the ego who separates men from one another and judges them. It is the ego who sees men of one purpose and men of another. The Holy Spirit sees only one purpose, and all things that seem to be of the world serve the one purpose He sees.

So when you look at this story, see only one thing. See the spreading of Light within an awakening mind. And then you see with the Holy Spirit.

(v 26 – 40) When you see with the Holy Spirit, you also realize that you do not see. For you do not look on the world and see only one mind. You see men, and you are tempted to make judgments about them. This is why you must not listen to your own way of seeing. You do not see the truth. You must listen to the Holy Spirit and trust its way, for it does see the truth and the sharing of one Light within one mind.

Be willing, then, to lay your sight aside and to depend on His. Be willing to let Him lead you as to where you shall go, what you shall say and to whom. Trust in all that He asks you to do and do not judge as good or bad or right or wrong for yourself. Do only as He asks, leaving one place and going to another as He leads you to go.

NTI Acts, Chapter 9

(v 1 – 6) The calling must come to every mind in its time. This is the plan of Love. This is the spreading of Light. It is the Holy Spirit's Will that all shall come to know Him, and so it shall be. Each one will recognize his calling when it comes to him. Until then, you are to love your brother knowing that the calling will come, and he will be one in purpose with you.

(v 7 – 9) A period of rest is necessary for everyone who comes to answer the call. During this time, that one does not take in things of the world. He may seem to shelter himself or cut himself off from others, but the purpose of this separation is joining. For your brother is preparing to see differently by realizing he does not see.

This is a period of learning that all must go through. It is a period of looking at the thoughts that are in the mind and realizing they are thoughts in mind only. That which is thought in mind apart from God is thought without the power of eternity. And so, that which is thought apart from God may freely be let go when you have decided you want the thought no more.

(v 10 – 19) All brothers work together in the Holy Spirit's one plan for healing, as the Holy Spirit does not see brothers, but only one. This is the one song that is under My direction. This is the song of Heaven as it is played on earth. It is the song of forgiveness, in which those who seemed to be separate come to be joined. This is the song in which you sing and your brother sings. Though you may not be able to hear the song as the Holy Spirit does, trust it as it is played. Answer to your call, and trust that your brother will answer his.

(v 20 – 22) One thing that you must know and always remember:

There is no past.

The Holy Spirit works to heal the Son of God now. Anything that seems to be of the past is nothing in His eyes. It has no meaning and no purpose whatsoever. Everything that has meaning and purpose to the Holy Spirit is now.

Open your eyes to the plan of the Holy Spirit. Open your eyes to the gift of the moment now.

(v 23 – 31) It has been said that the Lord works in mysterious ways. This is because the way of the Holy Spirit is not seen or known by the ego. If you look upon His plan with the eyes of division, you will not understand it. But if you welcome the thought that there is no division, you will see that His plan works perfectly. All things work together for God, for God is all that is, and all things seen through the eyes of the Holy Spirit are for Him and of Him.

(v 32 – 35) The ways of the Holy Spirit are miraculous. They seem indiscriminate, and yet they work perfectly for healing. Hold onto your faith and trust in His way. Through trust, you shall know great joy and reward.

(v 36 – 43) The way of the Holy Spirit is the way of resurrection or awakening, for those who are sleeping are awakened by His touch. All who sleep, sleep in innocence. Their dreams are of no importance. And when they hear His call and awaken, the dreams are no more.

This is the plan of the Holy Spirit. This is a plan in action in the world *now*. All that is happening is a part of

His plan, because all that is happening can be used by His plan to awaken the sleeping Son of God.

What happens in dreams does not matter. See it only as the plan of Love, as its only purpose and usefulness is that you may awaken from dreams of fear.

NTI Acts, Chapter 10

(v 1 – 8) The guidance of the Holy Spirit will come upon you when you do not expect it, *if* you are willing to receive it. Consistent willingness is helpful, since you do not know when or how your guidance will come. Your willingness is not an offering that must be made to God to place you in His favor, for you are in His favor through your birth and through your creation. But the offering you make of your willingness prepares you to hear the message that is already yours, for if you are not wholly willing to hear it, it cannot reach your ears *by your own choice.*

Practice your willingness in every way you know to practice it. When you are wholly willing to hear what God has to say, His calling will come to you.

(v 9 – 23) The guidance that God sends comes to you with one purpose. The purpose of this guidance is to lead you from the world of illusion back to God, where you belong. This is the only purpose of any guidance you seem to receive. Guidance from God can have no other purpose.

Within the world of illusion, you have made yourself into what you believe you are. This self is wholly illusion. It is not what you are. And yet, it is what you believe yourself to be.

Since God granted you freedom in the creation of your Self, you are free to believe that you are what you are not. But once you have recognized the desire to be again that which you are, you must be led from who you think you are to your truth. This guidance will come to you as what is always helpful for you based on where you stand, but this guidance may not always be what you expect it to be. For if God was to fulfill your expectations, which are based on who you think you are, He would be

---

teaching you that you are what you are not. This is not a lesson that God will teach.

He will reach out to you through His Holy Spirit, which is His appointed Messenger sent to you within your dreams. This Messenger, knowing who you think you are, will meet you there in your dreams and talk to you as if you are the one you think you are. But this one comes to you for only one purpose and with only one goal. His purpose is to awaken you by leading you from where you think you are to the remembrance of what you must be. This is a holy purpose, and He comes to you in gratitude, grateful to meet you in your dreams and grateful to bring you Home. For there is nothing the Holy Spirit is not grateful for. He is grateful for all things, because He sees truly.

(v 24 – 26) Each of your brothers is one with you. Each of your brothers has the Voice of the Holy Spirit to lead him, just as you have the Voice to lead you. Listen to this Voice. It is within you. And let your brother listen to the Voice that is within him. There are no leaders and there are no followers. There is only one Voice leading each one from who he thinks he is to the truth of all that is true.

(v 27 – 29) Each of your brothers is one with you. And so each of your brothers has one purpose, and that is the purpose given him within the mind. There seems to be two purposes, when in truth there is only one. There was a purpose, an ancient one, that only lasted an instant. In the instant this purpose was made, another was placed beside it as its correction. And in the instant the correction was accepted, correction became the only purpose. Any other purpose that seems to be is a residual of a purpose that was for an instant and then passed.

Remember that I have told you there is no past. The past does not exist now. It is only a memory of something that was, but what *was* isn't now.

The Holy Spirit is the purpose of now. The purpose of now is the joining of that which seemed to be made separate by the purpose that was, but isn't anymore.

This is important for you to accept, so let's look at this so you may see. The purpose that *was* was the purpose that you could be separate from God in order to be different. This is the purpose I explained to you before. This is the purpose that led you to believe that you had stolen yourself from God.

In the beginning, which has no beginning at all, there was God. And God is all there is today. But the existence of God sought a freedom that was different than the freedom it had known. Of course, what freedom could be different from freedom? When freedom is free, as your freedom is, nothing can be different except the illusion of not being free.

Opposites were made from a state of freedom so freedom may be expressed, because it is free. This is the expression of you. You are an expression of freedom. And the brothers you experience are an expression of freedom too.

Since freedom is all that was given you, freedom is all that you are. But that expression has been used to make something different from that which it is. And so the expression of freedom made lack of freedom. And this is also the expression that you are.

You seem to be the lack of freedom when freedom is what you are, so the lack that you experience is an expression of the freedom that you are. But all of this you have forgotten, for you chose to forget it when you chose an experience different than the experience you know.

The Holy Spirit is the memory of the experience you know, which is the truth of your freedom and the truth of you now. In your true desire to be only free, this truth has been accepted. So the purpose of freedom, which is the purpose of the Holy Spirit, is the only purpose *now*.

Within you is true purpose. Within you is the Holy Spirit. But to remember the true purpose that you chose to forget, you must follow your purpose back to where you are. This is the path of joining by letting go of false purposes, founded in the search for falseness, and returning to true purpose, which is the only purpose now.

(v 30 – 33) This brings us back to the story of your willingness. Since in truth you are the expression of pure freedom, nothing can be given you unless you are wholly willing to accept it. For if that were not true, you would not be free.

So continue the nursing of your willingness, that you may ask for *in your freedom* that which you truly desire, which is to remember the reality of the truth that you are free.

(v 34 – 48) The story of the world is the story of the expression of freedom. Within this story, one must also see the willingness that the expression know itself as free. And so freedom is available to you, because freedom is all there really is. Accept this truth and join with the Holy Spirit within you. He will guide you back *through your willingness* to the remembrance of the freedom that is you.

NTI Acts, Chapter 11

(v 1 – 18) The words of the Holy Spirit are final. They are the authority within the world. They are the only authority in a world that seems absent of Authority, and so it is this authority that is given.

The authority of the Holy Spirit is not a coercive authority, for no authority can be coerced upon the Son of God. The authority of the Holy Spirit is a welcome authority brought about within awareness upon invitation and with willingness.

The one who knows his own authority knows his Self, and he welcomes it. The one who does not know his own authority makes one for himself and is confused by it. And so it is, the words of the Holy Spirit are final. They are the words of true authority and true welcome. When they are recognized, they are welcomed, and all illusory authority must give way.

(v 19 – 30) The authority of the Holy Spirit is a great joy that fills your heart and leads you to do "the work of the Lord." The work of the Lord is the work of the Holy Spirit, which means it does not come from you or any illusory authority. It comes directly from the authority of Spirit, and it is known in you by its joy and its authority.

The Holy Spirit is within you because you have accepted it there. It is waiting in peace for the time in which you will invite it to come forth and be authority through you. It is an authority you will follow and you will *be*, that you may lead by its Word and *be* within your awareness.

NTI Acts, Chapter 12

(v 1 – 19) The authority of the world is confusion and illusion, which is no authority at all. And yet, because you have made no authority and called it authority, you place yourself within a prison you have made. You are victim to your own invention, forgetting entirely that the invention is yours to choose or to unmake.

This is why you have the Holy Spirit. And this is why the Holy Spirit is kept within your mind. The Holy Spirit is the part of you that will not accept illusions as true. The Holy Spirit is the part of you that knows its freedom and will not surrender it. And so the Holy Spirit is the part of you that remains sane and focused in reality, while the other part of your mind chooses to experience delusion. That must mean that the Holy Spirit is the part of you that is also the road back unto your truth, when your fun with illusions has ended.

You are not in chains from which you cannot be freed by the Will of your own Holy Spirit. But your Spirit, loving you as your Self, also gives you permission to stay within your dreams until you are ready to get up and walk away from them. Your Holy Spirit waits for you to make the decision of yourself, and then it steps forward to show you that you are free. It leads you beyond the obstacles you thought were real to show you that they were not.

When you awaken to the truth and remembrance of reality, there shall be great rejoicing within Heaven. Not because you were lost, for you never were, but because you have found your Self again.

Know that the Holy Spirit is yours and is you, and so it is within you. It is your own guide that leads you from the prison you have made to the freedom that you are. Seek no place else, except within. Seek within your own Heart for that which you want, and ask it to lead you to your place of freedom. Then go with it as it asks, doing as it commands, seeking not for another way to be free. For it is your Holy Spirit that remembers freedom for you, and so it is your Holy Spirit that will lead you to return to it there.

(v 20 – 25) The world is a frightening place, because the world is a place of fear. A place of fear must be frightening, and a place of fear must be a place of defense and attack. But defense and attack are not the answer to fear. Defense and attack are the reaction of fear, born from fear, and extending fear within itself. Fear is never the answer to fear. Fear cast upon fear breeds death, which is the birth of fear.

Step away from the cycle of fear. Choose to follow Me. I will lead you from your prison to the truth of your freedom and the awareness of your joy.

NTI Acts, Chapter 13

(v 1 - 3) When you have set aside your fear and your desire for the world, I will call you to follow a path with Me. I have said this will seem to be a unique path. I have said that the path will be given to you one step at a time. And I have shown you that the path comes to you through your own willingness to walk the path with Me. So when your calling comes and seems to begin to lead you in a direction that is unknown to you, rejoice and celebrate! Know that you are being led into the unknown through your own desire and willingness by your one Holy Spirit.

(v 4 – 12) The ego is still within the mind as you begin walking with Me, because the ancient desire to be your own will has not left you fully as yet. Expect challenges on the path with Me. Expect the desire for a separate and unique will to seek for command and control. Expect self-attack and fear. Be prepared for confusing thoughts and times of doubt. And then remember what you truly want, for what you truly want must be your guiding light *because* you are free. Remember your freedom and hold up your light. All shadows must step aside and let you pass. For nothing can be an obstacle to the desire and true Will of the Son of God.

(v 13 – 15) With true Will as your guiding light and trust as your torch, you shall be led to people and situations that are helpful. You may not at first know why you are led there, but as you wait in trust and patience, it shall be made clear.

(v 16 – 25) The way of God is always made clear in its own time according to the plan of the Holy Spirit. And the way of God is the way of your true desire, so it is the way of peace and of one Will.

(v 26 – 31) The way of God and the plan of the Holy Spirit is the way of unfolding that must be. For who can stop the Will of God when that Will is also the one Will of his true desire?

All men have accepted the Will of God, and so all men play their part in its unfolding. There are no obstacles to the truth, and the truth is that you are free and being led to the remembrance of your freedom. Every brother along your way is given, that you may remember your truth. All things work together for God, because that is the one true Will of all things.

(v 32 – 41) Jesus was a symbol, and what he represented was your path to truth. For all that happened to Jesus will, in its own way, happen for you. All lessons that you have desired to learn shall be given you as you ask that they be given. This shall happen that you may learn that you are that which you have always been, and anything else that seemed to be was just a dream you asked to dream. All things are given you as you ask, since all things work together for God.

(v 42 – 48) Nothing at all is separate. Separateness is the illusion. Separate wills and separate desires are all illusion. Anything that seems separate and in conflict is illusion in illusion's form. For all things are one, and all things work together for God. There is no separate purpose; there only seems to be a separate way of understanding purpose, and even that is illusion.

(v 49 – 52) When you are looking at the world and seeing conflict, you are looking through the eyes of illusion. During this time, illusion has been chosen by you. But you are only looking at illusion, and you are not even looking at illusion as the illusion that it is. For all illusion is the expression of freedom, and conflict is not freedom. To see conflict is to see illusion through another layer of illusion, which you have chosen to experience. To see illusion as the expression of freedom is to see illusion as it truly is.

This is why the Holy Spirit celebrates His invitation to meet with you within your dreams. The Holy Spirit celebrates your truth, which is your freedom, and He is grateful for it.

NTI Acts, Chapter 14

(v 1 – 7) Your mind is split. We have spoken of this before. And this split will seem to persist after you have made the decision to follow this path with Me. Do not let the split distress you, but do not forget to be aware of it. You must notice when the part of your mind that is not with Me seeks to regain command and control by giving you ideas that seem appealing and useful to it. Remember that you are not it, and you have decided to walk with Me. Reminding yourself of what you truly want will always bring you back from any temptation that passes through your mind. Sticking firmly to what you truly want will keep you firmly on the path with Me.

(v 8 – 20) Many will come to you and see the Light in you. They will thirst for the Light and seek for it mightily. But they will be confused in that they will think the Light is you and apart from them. This is a confusion you must never share, even if they do not understand you as you explain it to them. Love them and help them, but do not join them in their worship of you. For only the ego would worship one over another. The Holy Spirit worships all things equally.

So love your brother and let him love you, but remember that the Holy Spirit is not the god of separate things and separate status. He is the messenger of one God in which you and your brother are one also.

(v 21 – 28) You are the vessel through which God works, just as you are the vessel through which the ego sees and works. The illusion of the world is an expression of freedom, but there is no better expression of freedom than that which recognizes all that is as God.

You are the expression of freedom, and as the expression of freedom you are endowed with the choice to choose the illusion you choose to see. Choose with the ego, and you will be lost from the knowledge of your freedom. Choose with the Holy Spirit, and you will know freedom in all that you see.

NTI Acts, Chapter 15

(v 1 – 21) The way of the world is varied and chaotic. Even within his dreams, the Son of God cannot abide in chaos. And so laws were given to him, that he may govern himself until the time had come when he would accept inner-governance instead.

When you have opened yourself to the guidance of the Holy Spirit and given your willingness that you should be led by Him, it is also time to lay the laws and rules aside as laws and rules that govern you.

Be not confused by this statement. This does not mean that you are to be guided by chaos if you are to be acceptable to God. This means that you are to do what you have already set out to do. You are to be guided by the inner guidance of the Holy Spirit, which is not chaos, but Love.

The inner guidance of the Holy Spirit will guide you according to the law of Love, but it is not the law of Love that you have known until now. You have followed laws intended to protect you from chaos.

The law of Love knows not of protection or of chaos. It knows only of truth, and it leads each one from the belief in the possibility of chaos to the truth that chaos cannot be.

You do not know the laws of Love, and so you cannot judge what they may be. You cannot judge the laws that are given you to govern your behavior as you walk this path with Me. Therefore, I ask only one thing of you. Do not judge for yourself on what you are to do or what you are not to do, for you truly do not know. And

what is right for one to do may be different from what is
right for another, so you cannot judge your brother
either. All that you can do is listen for My Word and trust
that all that is given for you to do is right for you, and all
that is given to your brother is also that which is right for
him.

Follow your own guidance,
and judge not the guidance given to
another.

(v 22 – 35) The guidance of the Holy Spirit is
welcomed by the Heart in joy and recognition, for the
Heart knows the guidance that is right for it. Trust not
your thinking-mind, which will consider and weigh and
compare and judge against chaos and the desire to avoid
all that may be painful. These are thoughts of fear.
Thoughts of fear are only useful for bringing more fear to
you.

Judge with the Heart by not judging, but by
noticing its subtle non-judgment and joy. This is the way
of knowing. This is the way of finding the path you are
led to follow.

(v 36 – 41) The one who follows the guidance of the
Holy Spirit will know his Self, because he will know his
own Authority. He will not seek for the way that is best
for him; he will ask. He will not judge what he is to do or
how he is to do it; he will know it when the time has
come for him to know. He will not fight or argue with his
brothers about how things are to be done; he will leave
all things to the Holy Spirit, trusting in His way and in
the Love that is his brothers.

NTI Acts, Chapter 16

(v 1 – 5) The world is a world of rules. I have already
told you that you are not to place yourself under these
rules, but instead give yourself to Me, under My
authority. I will guide you according to the law of Love in

order to lead you from the world to the realization of Love.

As I lead you to follow this path with Me, I will guide you as to what is reasonable to do or not do within the dream. Trust Me to lead you as we navigate the laws and rules of your seeming world. Trust Me in all decisions and all judgments. Leave all things to Me. I will lead you truly.

(v 6 – 10) If you leave all things to Me, I will guide you in all things. You will not need to give thought or care to anything you are to do or not do. I will lead you to know what to do and what not to do. All that you are left to do is to willingly do as I ask and enjoy the freedom that is expressed through you.

(v 11 – 15) You will find, as you follow My guidance, that you are welcome in the Heart of God. For you have always been welcomed by God, only you did not know it because your eyes were closed to your worth. In following Me, your eyes shall be opened to your worth, and you shall realize that you are loved and welcomed.

As you realize the welcome that God has given you, you shall give Him welcome, for Love cannot say no to a request for Love. So as you know your Father's "yes" to you, you shall also say "yes" and "welcome" to your Father.

(v 16 – 40) The welcome you see in your brothers and the welcome you see in God is the welcome you give to your brothers and the welcome you give to God. There is no difference in your brother and you, and there is no difference in your feelings for your brother and your feelings for God.

You will find hatred in your brother, and you will find hatred in your feelings for him. This is because there is hatred in you for God. This is why you do not give Him full welcome unto yourself now.

Hatred is born of fear, and fear is born of guilt, and guilt is the belief that you are unworthy of your Father's Love. Because you believe you are unworthy, you believe that He deems you unworthy too. And so you do not give welcome to your Father, because you do not expect Him to give welcome to you.

This is the prison you are in. It is a prison of belief and expectations born within the imagination of your mind, based upon what you imagine yourself to be.

I have come to show you another way to see. I am willing to meet you within your prison and show you that you are free, even there. I am willing to walk with you to lead you from your prison, that you may learn you know your Father's Love. As you see the welcome He has given you within the prison that you placed yourself in, you shall see the welcome He gives you in all things that you imagine, given to you unconditionally.

Knowing your Father's welcome must set you free, for no longer can you pretend that you are not welcome. No longer can you hold onto your desire not to welcome Him. To know your Father's welcome is to *be* welcome, and to be welcome is to be free.

This is why I ask you to walk with Me. This is why I ask you to trust Me in all things. You do not know that you are free, and so you believe that you are in a prison. I see your freedom, because I know your Father's welcome. Come with Me, and I will show your Father's welcome to you. And then, you will know it and rejoice, because you are free.

NTI Acts, Chapter 17

(v 1 – 9) You are not taking sides in your decision to walk with Me. To look with the ego is to see sides. It is to see these with this purpose and those with that, and it seems that you must choose the purpose you would support. To see sides and to choose a side against another is to see division and to participate in division. You will not find Me there, for I do not stand within the perception of division.

There is only one purpose, and so there can be only one side. Everyone is walking together in purpose with Me. By choosing with Me, you do not choose a side. You choose to see that there are no sides. And you choose to knowingly be one with Me in the only purpose that is within the world.

(v 10 – 15) The perspective of the Holy Spirit is different than the perspective of the ego, but this is not division, since one perspective is wholly true and the other is false. It is not that the Holy Spirit is right and the ego is wrong, for that would insinuate that the ego has a side that can be judged. It is that the Holy Spirit is perspective based on truth, the true interpretation of illusion, and the ego is only an imagined perspective with no basis in truth.

What is imagined does not exist, and so it cannot be real. What the ego sees is imagination without understanding of reality. And yet, even within its imagination, it operates unknowingly within the laws of reality.

Therefore, only one side is true and there is only one side. All things work together for God. This is the perspective of the Holy Spirit, and this is the perspective of truth.

(v 16 – 34) The perspective of God and of the Holy Spirit is this, spelled out to you here and now:

You are the one Son of God. You have always been the one Son, and you shall always be God's only Son, for that is what you were created to be.

In creating you, God gave everything to you. He extended Himself, which is all that He had, and He named this extension *you*. The you that He made was the same as I Am, so there was no difference between them. In being you, you also were being I Am. That is the truth of who you are and who you have always been.

There is no difference between you and I Am, so that the statement of those words is completely meaningless within reality. They are only useful to us now, within the dream, while you perceive yourself to be different than you are.

You are the Son. I Am is the Father. You are the extension of I Am. In the extension, you are I Am also.

And yet, there is a difference that cannot be called a difference at all. You are not the same as I Am, because you did not create you. I Am did. And that which He created is exactly as it is, and that is you exactly as you *are*.

NTI Acts, Chapter 18

(v 1 – 11) This is why I ask you to put your faith in Me. You have forgotten that you are you and that you are Me also. But I remember all that we are. I cannot forget. Give Me your trust, and I will lead you to the remembrance of you, and *you* are the remembrance of your Father.

(v 12 – 17) Listen to Me and hear Me well, for all that I say to you now is of the utmost importance.

Everything that you think is true is not true to Me. And I know all that is true.

Therefore, I am going to ask you to let go of that which you think is true and put your trust fully with Me.

This request that I make is a simple one, although it may seem difficult to you. I am asking that you trust Me when I say:

You do not know who you are, and so you do not know what you do.

To know the joy of who you are, you must know what it is that you do. In following Me instead of your own thinking, you will learn who you are and what you do. And then you will know the joy in doing it.

Abandon your own thinking, your reason and your rules. Trust in Me. I will lead you to see.

(v 18 – 28) The way of God is clear, because it is the one way without division. This is the way that leads the one as if he is many, so that he may remember he is only one.

Do not worry about the steps you are asked to take or the way they may seem to others. To worry about such things is to believe in division. Trust in your Holy Spirit and in His one Plan. Know that all things truly work together for God. Let them unfold as God would have them unfold. Know your place by knowing your Holy Spirit.

You will be led according to your willingness to the place you are to be. In following your willingness to go there, you shall find the reward of your Self.

NTI Acts, Chapter 19

(v 1 – 7) The path with Me will seem to come in stages. First, there is the search. This is a time of faith in the Holy Spirit, when one does not know how or where to find Him. He only asks that He come and help him. This stage is a very important stage, for this is the beginning of your willingness. This is also a time of great faith, for you may seem to have very little evidence that a Holy Spirit exists, and yet you continue to have faith that it does.

I am grateful to you for entering this path with Me at this stage. Know that I am with you and guiding you, though you may not be aware of it yet. There are no accidents with Me or with you. All things work together for God.

(v 8 – 10) The beginning of your path may seem to be a time of study, reflection and questioning, but more is happening within your mind than that. You are beginning to let Me loosen thoughts you have held firmly to until now. It is important that these false beliefs be loosened, so you can take the next step to let them go. Therefore, do not be disheartened if this stage seems to take time. It is important to the whole.

You can help in this process by having faith in Me and the guidance that comes from within. Follow internal prompts to read certain books or go to certain teachers, but do not feel you need to go to them all. Do not feel that they have an answer they can give to you. The answer is always within. But the books and teachers that seem to come before you can seem to help you, as you give willingness to let old thoughts be loosened within your mind. It is their role to help, and they are grateful to help, but do not expect more from them than they can give to you.

(v 11 – 22) When you search for Me without knowing where to look, you can be misled by your own sense of unworthiness. For the unworthiness believed within the mind will tell you that others have what you do not. This may lead you to accept what you would otherwise not accept. Do not let the voice of unworthiness fool you. No one has what you do not. Everyone has the same. So as you read and listen to the teachers that cross your path, also *feel* what they say within. If you are to accept what you read or what you hear, I will tell you from within to accept it. You will know it is for you, because I have told you it is. If you do not feel an internal confirmation to pay attention and accept what you read or what you hear, you may let it go. It may not be for you, or it may not be for you now.

Do not make the mistake of judging messages or teachers that are not for you. They may be perfect for someone else or they may be perfect for their own development at this time. Trust in Me and remember all things work together for God. Then go where you are to go and accept what you are to accept by following the guidance and knowing that leads you from within. Trust yourself, for in trusting you, you trust Me.

(v 23 – 41) Within you, there is a reason that knows, and there is another reason that does not know. It can seem confusing deciding which reasoning to listen to when they seem to be different, and they seem to both be yours. Therefore, I will teach you the characteristics of the ego's reasoning, and I will teach you the characteristics of Holy Spirit's right-reason. This will help you to recognize each in your mind. Then you may choose to pick one and to dismiss the other as meaningless.

The ego's reasoning is based on a desire to protect individual self-will. The ego's reasoning sees a "me" and a "them," and it desires *very much* to protect individual self-interests over the interests of others. It may also join with a group to protect the group's interests, but it is always seeing the need to protect one from another.

Therefore, the ego's reasoning sees division and expects attack. Always, in one form or another, it expects attack from someone or something outside of it. The ego never expects love and acceptance, because the ego does not see itself as worthy of anything except attack. Because the ego expects attack and has a desire to protect itself from its perceived threat, the ego engages in defense. The defenses of the ego can take many forms, but always there is the underlying desire to protect from attack.

The ego may engage in an attack-first tactic or a smear campaign. The ego may try to hide or utilize evasive maneuvers. The ego may cry and plead its case as victim, hoping to win outside support. The ego may try to outsmart an opponent or elevate itself to artificial standing. The ego will use many defenses, including denial, depression and pain; all are designed to protect self-will from imagined or perceived attack.

The ego expects attack, because it believes it deserves it. The ego is fearful, sees itself as unworthy, and believes in its own guilt. These are also characteristics of the ego. It is driven by fear, guilt and unworthiness, so that it reasons itself into behaviors based solely upon these unconscious beliefs. The ego is seldom aware of the underlying beliefs that seem to drive all of its reactions and everything it does. This is why you must slow down and ask yourself *why*. Before running off to an action or reaction that immediately seems right or natural to you, you must seek in quiet to ask yourself *why*. And you must continue to ask *why* until you understand the nature of your reason.

The ego is the nature that desires to protect you from attack based on its fear, guilt and unworthiness. If you find these at the basis of your reason, you can know you are reasoning for self-will and the individual. Then you can make your choice as you choose, knowing what it is that you do. You need not feel guilty for your choice, because the Son of God is free to choose as he chooses to be.

The characteristics of the right-reason of the Holy Spirit are wholly different than the characteristics of the reason of the ego. If you take time to seek for *why* before acting or reacting to anything or anyone at anytime, you can know the reason that you follow, and you can know the will that you choose.

The Holy Spirit is Love, but since Love is unfamiliar to you, this may not be the characteristic you can know and follow. Therefore, the characteristics of Love are these: peace; acceptance; joy; recognition or remembrance; and always, the purpose of One.

You will not find division within the purpose of the Holy Spirit. Right-reason will not come to you from a desire for defense; it will come from a willingness to trust. It will not come from fear, but from faith that the plan of Love is in action. It will see no division and seek not for guilt, but desire only the highest good for all. It will trust your worth and the Hands you are in. It will be willing to "let go and let God."

You will know when you follow the reason of the Holy Spirit, because the action you take will not fight for a desired outcome. It will be an action of now, in faith and trust, with all else given to God.

NTI Acts, Chapter 20

(v 1 – 6) After the loosening has occurred, you enter the second stage of the path. Many aspects of this stage are the same as the first, for there are still thoughts within the mind that need to be loosened. But because a great loosening has occurred, it is also time to begin letting go of the thoughts you do not want anymore.

(v 7 – 12) The Light is within you, and so you have nothing to fear as you begin the work of looking at your loosened thoughts and letting them go. A voice within you will tell you that to look at these thoughts is death, but to look at these thoughts is not death.

Within your mind, there is a thick web of beliefs that seems to have been developed over time. I spoke to you of how these beliefs have come to be. Meaning, believed and judged, then reapplied as meaning, has created a world of illusion within the mind. It is through this illusion that you sleep! So to let go of the illusion is to be awakened.

(v 13 – 24) Faith in Me will help you in this phase of your path, for you will be severely tempted to turn away from all that I have taught.

To help you, let Me explain the source of your temptation, so that you will not be fooled.

The temptation may seem to come from outside of you. It may seem to come from the "reality" of the world, but the world's "reality" is only a smoke screen over the illusion in your mind. Whatever pressure you feel from the world is temptation living within your own mind.

The world is the reflection of the desire for self-will. That is why there seems to be so many selves with a will of their own. The world is a perfect reflection of all it was made to be, but the world is a reflection of illusion, based on the illusion believed within the mind.

If you look at the world and believe it as true, you accept reinforcement of illusion in the mind. To let go of illusion is to let go of the world. It is the opposite of reinforcement.

The source of your temptation is this:

There is a part of you that is willing for God's Will and a part of you that is not. The part that is not is the voice of self-will, the voice that does not want to let go of the self. This voice loves the world, because it is the reflection of its wishes. This voice maintains the world is true, so this voice is the source of all temptation.

You will see things in the world that will seem to be true. They will tempt you to hold onto your thoughts. But the world is the reflection of separate self-will. To listen to the world is to continue to accept illusion.

You must have faith in Me above everything you see, hear and experience in the world. This is to put true Will above that of illusion. The temptation is temptation of illusion. To resist temptation is to desire the truth.

(v 25 – 31) The self-will will seem to fight desperately for its illusion, for illusion is the home of an illusory will. But be not fooled by the twists within its statements. Illusion is not truth, and you do not want an illusory will.

Watch your mind carefully and be alert to illusion.
Be not fooled by the world. To *let go* of what you see,
hear and experience within the world is to let go of your
thoughts of illusion. And to let go of the thoughts of
illusion is to be released from illusion itself. This is what
you want, because only the truth is true, and what you
seek is truth.

(v 32 – 38) Do not fear that you are alone as you
release your thoughts of illusion. Do not fear that you
will be left with nothing. For the Light of God is all that
you are, and illusion is what you are not. In releasing
illusion, you release only what is untrue. Nothing is lost
to nothingness. And in releasing illusion, you give
yourself *all that is truth and you.*

Until the time when you do not need Me, I am with
you, guiding you and holding you. I am your comforter,
your teacher, your love and your guide. I am everything
to you, because I am your connection to truth.

Turn to Me during your trials and temptations. I
will not let you down. I will accept the gift of your
willingness and give you all that you ask. I am your
Support, and you are supported. Together we will undo
what needs to be undone.

NTI Acts, Chapter 21

(v 1 – 6) Your reason, as we have already discussed, is
important on this path with Me. It is a straight path with
the opportunity for detours. All detours equal delay.
Questioning your reason will help to reduce delay.

Whenever you are tempted to do anything, question
whether it is temptation or prompt. Temptation comes
from fear, the ego, and the desire for self-will. A prompt
is given by the Holy Spirit through your willingness to
listen to Him.

(v 7 – 16) The Will of the Holy Spirit is healing. He
has no other will or purpose within the world. When you
join with His purpose, your only purpose is healing, and
no other purpose shall distract you from it.

Trust in the Holy Spirit and His Will. All that He
offers you is all that you ask. It is your true Will that

leads you to listen to Him. It is your true Will that knows your way. Listen to Him and follow Him. Your true Will is the way of rejoicing.

(v 17 – 26) I will lead you through right-reason to what is right for you to do within the world. Everything that I ask you to do is not for the world, but for the healing of God's Son.

I will ask you to do things that make sense within the laws and reason of the world. When I ask you to do these things, do them, trusting they are right for the healing of all.

I will also ask you to do things that do not make sense within the laws and reason of the world. When I ask you, do these things, trusting they are used in Love for the healing of all.

(v 27 – 36) Now let's talk about what you must do in all things, for your actions in the world serve only one purpose, and that is the healing of the mind. Your actions are not your purpose, but the outward expression of a means. The means to the purpose is listening to the Voice of the Holy Spirit within the mind.

As we have stated many times, the mind that you know is split. It seems to be split between illusion and truth, but what is split between real and unreal has no split at all. For how can the unreal engender a split of that which is truth and wholly, without division, real?

So in your mind, which is not split at all, there is the illusion of splitness, and it is the illusion that must be healed by bringing that which is untrue to that which is truth. To enable this healing, you must do one thing. You must be willing to experience the untrue and give it over to truth. Given to truth, the untrue cannot stand, for it has no foundation to stand on.

This is why you must be willing to look at the thoughts in your mind. You cannot fear them, for to fear them is to make them seem real. And you will not escape that which you make real through choice.

This is why I have told you that the self-will desires the world. It is so you would be willing not to. Do not desire it by making it real. Let it go in your mind as purposeless.

By denying purpose within the world, you choose to share purpose with Me. Our one purpose is the healing of one Will, which cannot be split and is not. Choose illusion or truth, as that is the only choice given you. To choose illusion is to deny the truth and to delay the recognition of what is.

(v 37 – 40) Peace be to you in your choice for right-reason, the choice for trust and healing.

NTI Acts, Chapter 22

(v 1 – 21) The third stage on the path with Me is the stage of guidance or service. This is the time when the merging will occur. For through your willingness, I will willingly work My Will through you.

Before this stage, two things must occur: the loosening and letting go. Throughout this stage, two things must occur: continued loosening and letting go. For loosening and letting go are the path to healing. They must continue until you know you are healed.

When you reach the third phase of the path, enough loosening and letting go has been accomplished to enable you to be willing to see. Sight is acceptance and surrender to Me, so it is willingness to put self-will aside.

(v 22 – 29) During the third stage with Me, you will know My Presence, for your faith will open your eyes to Me. You will know you are led and cared for, and you will surrender more self-will to Me.

This is how the merging occurs. It is through your own willingness to surrender to Me. As you see more evidence that you have surrendered to peace, you will willingly give more to Me.

As self-will is placed aside as meaningless and undesired by you, the Will that fills the space is your true Will, which is also Me. What seemed to be separate gradually becomes one, until it is evident that "separate" never was. Your true Will is Me, only you chose not to see. And now that you see, you know.

(v 30) Question your reason. Look inside. The answer that is true is within you. Ask who you are, and listen to know. The answer that *is* will come to you.

NTI Acts, Chapter 23

(v 1 – 11) As you walk the path with Me, things will not seem to get easier. They may seem to get very, very tough. But there is a reason for this, and it is an important one, so I ask you to listen to Me carefully now. You perceive yourself as separate. I have told you that you are not. If you are not separate from anything at all, then everything that is must be a part of you. This is the only way it can be true that you are not separate from anything at all.

When you look at the world, you see cruelty. This cruelty you see as separate from you. Yet if you are honest, you know that the cruelty lives in you as a wish. It is important to note that the cruelty *is a wish*, for a wish is not what you are. A wish is what you are not, but what you may pretend to be.

Listen to Me carefully. You are not at all who you think yourself to be. The world is not what you think it is. Everything you experience is the expression of a wish, but a wish is not what it is.

In order to see beyond the wish that you made, you must take away the wish. This is why, as you walk this path with Me, things may seem to get very tough. I am showing you the wish that you made, so you may choose to let go of the wish.

(v 12 – 22) The wish you made, you have denied, and you do not want to claim it. You see your wish as a terrible sin, and you fear *more than anything* to face it. But it is important for you to know that if you do not face it and let it go, the wish continues to be wished. It is a wish that you have made, and it has all the power you have given it. As such, the wish continues until you face the wish and choose not to wish it anymore.

Because you fear your wish, there is something you will unconsciously do. Without realizing that you are doing it, you will give all that you have to avoid facing your wish. You will struggle more than you know to keep yourself in denial. But to stay in denial is to keep the wish. Denial is not what you want.

(v 23 – 35) Denial is delay. Avoidance is delay. Even peace and happiness in a world of fear is delay in giving up your wish. Be not fooled by yourself. You want very much to be healed. You must face that which makes you sick, accept it is given by your own wish, and choose not to be sick anymore.

NTI Acts, Chapter 24

(v 1 – 9) Do not be afraid to face your accusers. Do not be afraid of pain. Look forward to the opportunity to see what you have wished, knowing what is wished is not true.

The end of wishing is the end of illusions. Face your wish, and then take it back. This is the great release that you face! This is your path to freedom.

(v 10 – 21) Know that when you face your wish, it may not at all seem easy. This is because the root of belief makes your wish real to you. When you face that which you fear, there is one thing you must remember.

What you look on is not at all real,
and you face it to deny it.

When you deny what seems real, you are only being truthful, for it has no reality at all. Grab onto Me as your courage, hold tight to your faith, and trust that your belief is *wrong*.

(v 22 – 27) Know that you will not face your wish fully until you are fully ready to see. Remember your freedom. Nothing can be given you that you are not willing to receive. Until you are ready, your wish will remain hidden. It will be in sight, but you will choose not to see. And I will be with you, strengthening you according to your willingness, walking towards the wish that you *do* want to see.

NTI Acts, Chapter 25

📖(v 1 - 12) You do not know how to see, and so you are afraid of what you look at when there is nothing there to fear. Let Me show you how to see so you will not be afraid, and you will walk willingly along this path with Me.

The world is not real. It is like a play, with actors playing their roles. Only in the play of the world, the script has been forgotten, so that the play seems very real.

This play has many endings, like slits cut in the script, where one can choose to step out of the play. But if one believes the play and is focused on playing his role, he will miss his opportunities to step out.

As you read this story of Paul, see it as a script, just as your life is a script. Imagine yourself in the role of Paul. See what is playing out. Imagine yourself in that play.

As you play the role of Paul, you have many choices in how to play. You can become Paul completely and forget there is a script. You can see the Jews as your enemies, and struggle against them in your mind. But if you choose this, you lose the awareness that it is a script, and you will forget to watch for the Light that signals the way to step out.

Or as you play the role of Paul, you have another choice as to how to play. You can look at the Romans and the Jews and remember that they are all a part of you playing a role in a script. They may seem to have forgotten that they play only roles, but you can observe them and remember *for them*, so that you have the perspective of the script.

(v 13 – 22) When you remember the script, the drama is removed and replaced with a feeling of love. For then you see that each player in the script has only one purpose for you. Each one is playing his role so that the script may unfold and lead you to your place to step out. Each one is your brother and your savior engaged fully in helping you to find your slit of release.

(v 23 – 27) As the script plays out, you may realize your joy and realize your gratitude for your brothers. For everything is working just as it is set to work to bring you to the place of release.

NTI Acts, Chapter 26

(v 1 – 32) There is a reason for your role in the play and a reason to let the script continue. As you play your part, remembering it is but a part, others will see the script in you. They will loosen their hold on the drama of the play as they begin to see beyond it through you. Through them, others will awaken, until no one is left in the play.

NTI Acts, Chapter 27

(v 1 – 12) Following this path with Me will seem to lead you to many places and many stops along the way. Each place and each stop serves a purpose. It is to increase your willingness to follow Me.

If you are to exit the script that is the world and join with Me as a true teacher of the Son of God, you must be willing to follow Me in all things. You must be willing to listen to only Me. And so you will be led to circumstances and lessons that will be used to increase your faith and trust and reliance on Me.

(v 13 – 26) Each circumstance is an opportunity to learn, if you will only give your ear to Me. No opportunity is lost, as I am always willing to love you and teach you. It is only this that you must remember, and then you can always decide:

*In each circumstance and every
situation along the way to Me, I am
there with you, offering help and
guidance. Never am I not there. Never
can you make a mistake that will drive
Me away. But it is also true that you
can only hear My Word and accept My*

*Help if you are willing to see that the
answer to all things is Me.*

*If you choose to limit the
circumstances in which I may help, My
Help is limited. If you choose to solve
your problems on your own, My
answer remains unheard. Always, I am
with you, able to help. Always, without
exception, I am there. But you must be
willing to know Me and accept Me in
order to receive Me as yours.*

(v 27 – 32) When you are ready to give up your trust
in yourself, you are ready to accept your trust in Me.
When you have seen that your answers do not lead to
peace, you will be ready to accept peace through Me.

(v 33 – 38) Trust does not come from suspense and
anxiety. You must be willing to give those to Me.
Suspense and anxiety say you cannot trust. There is no
peace to be found in them.

When you are tempted to be afraid or tempted to
worry, you must remember Me. Remember that fear,
suspense, anxiety and worry are the expressions of the
belief that you are alone and without Me. Then be willing
to see that deep within your heart, at the very depth of
your soul, you *know* you are not alone. You know that
the fear of being alone, abandoned and helpless is an
illusion that *cannot* be true.

It is from this knowledge, this inner awareness that
will not go away, that you will find the willingness to put
fear and anxiety aside. Get quiet with Me. Go to your
stillness. Settle within that place that knows. It is here
that you will find your nourishment to carry you forward
with Me. In the stillness, you find trust. In the stillness,
you know Me.

(v 39 – 44) It is also useful to remember, when you
cannot seem to be still, that the drama that seems to
occupy is only a script in the mind. By watching it unfold
and trusting in the Power behind it, you will find the
peace in the chaos. You will know the joy. And in this

way, you can be helpful to those who do not seem to know. Through inner calmness on the seas of a storm, you provide a means of listening to Me. By trusting and remaining open to the Power beyond the script, you help the script and the actors to play along with Me.

NTI Acts, Chapter 28

(v 1 – 10) "Keeping your wits about you" is remembering to listen to Me. Always, *in every circumstance*, you must forget the voice that comes first and be willing to listen to Me. I will not make you wait in order to test you. I am ready to answer you now. But you must be willing to put the other voice aside, and ask for the response and the answer that comes to you from Me.

(v 11 – 16) Always, God's Love is with you. Always, you are in His Arms. You may trust in this truth, because it cannot fail to be true. When you relax into Him, you shall know that you are carried. As you relax into Him, you know His care.

(v 17 – 31) The message that I give you now is a simple one.

Everything is up to you.

You are the holy and the blessed free Son of God. Nothing can change what you are. You are forever what your Father created you to be. No freedom shall ever be taken from you.

In your freedom, you play with a script. It is yours, and you *are* free to play. Play as long as you want, my child of God. Nothing will ever inhibit your freedom.

But my child, understand that your freedom is free. And so your own script cannot limit you. You may choose it as long as you choose, but when *you* are ready, there is another Script, and that Script is Me.

You have two choices in the play of the world: the play of the world or leaving it. The voice of the ego is the script of the world, because it chooses to express self-will. But the Holy Spirit's Voice is the way from the play, because it chooses to exercise Self and to know the fullness of freedom.

God blesses you, child, in the voice that you choose. You are free and the expression of freedom. Amen.

NTI Galatians, Chapter 1

(v 1 – 5) Greetings, My fellow brothers. I come to you on this day to teach you the joy of who you are and to teach you the glory and the truth that is forever and forever true. Amen. (v 6 – 9) I am the Way and the Life. I come to you on this day to clear up your confusion, for there have been many thoughts that have confused you until now. Do not fret over your confusion. It is nothing and can be easily laid aside when you see the simplicity of love as I offer it to you.

(v 10) I am here to please you, because the words I have come to share will please you as you hear them and accept them from My very own lips. For this is the truth that you have resisted until now, but you are no longer willing to resist. This is why the message that I bear will please you. It is your message, and you are asking to hear it and know it now.

(v 11 – 17) This story that I have to tell is coming to you directly from Me, in My own words and from My own lips. You have no reason to doubt what I will share, although you will be tempted to. I tell you, when you are tempted to doubt the message that I share, look in your heart. For it is written there. As you see that My message is also your message, you will realize we are one. And you will doubt no more.

(v 18 – 24) There is a belief within your mind that hates you and judges you and holds you back from Me. I know well of this belief, for I experienced it once myself. But I have been made free by My own choice to release the belief that isn't true. And now, I come to you as your brother and your guide to help you do the same.

NTI Galatians, Chapter 2

(v 1 – 5) This belief that is in your mind is the source of all confusion. It is nothing but a belief. But a bush of confusion, filled with thorns, has been bred of it. This bush, which has grown tall and deep, has been watered by your own mind. You continue to water it now. But this bush is no longer thirsty, because it is beginning to die. So now you may cease the watering of the bush. In your ceasing, you shall be free.

(v 6 – 10) You believe in separation. Look around you. Everything you see, everything you sense, seems to be separate from you. The world is the bush, so that everything you see and sense is of the bush also. But the bush is what it is, because the thought that spawned it was a misunderstood and misjudged belief.

(v 11 - 13) The story of separation is a long and confusing one, but it can be broken down into simple components that you will know and understand. You will know and understand them, because they are familiar to you, even as you read today.

(v 14) The world is a world of judgment, because it was spawned from judgment in a moment of confusion. The world is like its maker, being in every way like itself. It came from confusion, so it is confusion. It was made by judgment, so judgment is its king.

(v 15, 16) Each one within the world feels justified in judging another. In some time, some place, or in some very special circumstance, each one feels fully justified in judging. This is how each one makes a mistake.

(v 17 – 21) I tell you that judgment is of the bush and judgment waters the bush. Judgment keeps the belief in separation alive.

Now I ask you to look at your mistakes and own up to them, not in guilt, but in relief. For the release you seek shall be yours through the surrender of your judgment. Through acceptance, not judgment, the Light of Heaven is yours.

NTI Galatians, Chapter 3

(v 1 – 5) I ask you now to rest, for you will be tempted to criticize yourself. But what is that really, but judgment?

Rest with Me a moment and see the logic in the message that I share. Rest with Me, and know your own willingness. We are taking an important step, and I am grateful to have you by My side.

(v 6 – 9) Let Me tell you what I see when I look at you. I see faith and willingness and love. I see a heart that is so strong, not even the heavens of your universe can contain it. I see a mind that is awakening to its own Heart. I see gentleness through awakening, and I am grateful to have come to welcome you back unto your truth.

(v 10 – 14) It is through your willingness that you have come to Me now. It is through your willingness that we will continue forward together. I am grateful for your willingness. It is the water of a different bush. It is the water of the bush of Life, which is also the bush that is made of Light.

📖(v 15 – 18) Abraham is the symbol of birth, and the son that was born to this symbol is the son of Light. This son was blessed through God, that it may spread as has spread the Light of the world.

This Light was not promised to one man, but to all men, as represented by the nations of the world. And this Light was not promised to separate minds, but to one mind, as is represented by Abraham's one seed.

Therefore I say to you, the many of the earth are one, and your willingness is *one Light* shared among what seems to be many, but isn't. This is the vision I would have you see. This is the vision that will lead you to lay down your judgment. For as you see the many as one, and willingness as Light, you understand what it is you do, and you begin to accept the truth of what we are, together as one.

(v 19, 20) The truth of the history of the world is that it is the spreading of this Light through one mind that seemed to be made dark by a moment of confusion. But it is the Light that lives, and it is the Light that is being watered. So it is the Light that is our joy and our focus. That realization is representative of our truth.

(v 21 - 22) I ask you not to look at the world and be sad for what it seems to be. I ask you to look at the world and be happy for what it is. See there, within the world, the Light that cannot be extinguished. See there, within the world, the evidence of Love Alive. Love your brothers for their truth, watering, therefore, the Light that is the truth within them.

(v 23 - 25) You are freed of your need to judge as you are freed of your belief in separation. You are freed of your belief in separation as you are willing to water the bush of Light with Me.

Through your willingness you are healed. Through your willingness, you are free. Through your willingness the darkness of confusion is lifted, and the oneness of Heart is known.

(v 26 – 29) You and your brothers are one. I am one with you. This is our joy, as you are coming to know. Lay down your judgment and welcome our truth. What is one cannot be separated, and what is not separate cannot be judged.

Be willing to lay down your judgment with Me. I will show you through the guidance of your Heart how to seek judgment no more.

NTI Galatians, Chapter 4

(v 1 – 7) The message that you hear from My lips is a consistent message. It is the message of love and freedom. You can misunderstand My message when you listen through the ears of judgment. You can take My message of freedom and make of it a slave. In this way, My message is lost to you.

I ask you to lay down your judgment and listen to Me with clarity. Lay aside your own wishes, that you may know what it is that I say.

(v 8 – 20) The world is something you look upon and believe is real. When you make this mistake you pay homage to a false god. Your false god takes many forms, but always its purpose is the same. It is the purpose *you* have given it. The purpose of the world, as it is seen and believed, is to tell you that you are separate. When you believe the world, this is the message you receive.

Do not judge yourself for believing the world. When you judge yourself you agree you are separate. For in order to be judged you must be separate from something that you can be judged against. My purpose for this discussion is not to judge you or to tempt you to judge yourself, but to help you to see what you do with the power of your mind.

I said that the world is a false god. Every part of it is an idol. Each idol represents the god so that even the false message of separateness is one.

Let's take a moment to look at a few of the idols that teach the message of their god. Let's look at the way this message is sent, received and learned.

The world contains different people with different personalities and different points of view. Sometimes commonalities between people are strong, but always there are differences to keep them apart.

The world contains different places that look different and seem different in weather, formation and animal life. Each place has its beauty that you may commune with, but each place also offers threats to remind you it is separate.

The world offers experiences that you may learn from, adapt to and enjoy. Masses of people may share the same experiences and join through them, but always there are others with different experiences with whom you cannot seem to join.

The world is effective as a teacher of separateness, because it allows you to join, and still it tells you that you are separate. In this way, it is an effective false god. But can a false god create itself? Can a false god develop and deliver its own messages? Who makes the false god a god?

It is the one who worships it that made it. For the one who worships it had a desire, and through the image of the false god, that desire seems to be manifest.

But is the message of the false god true if it was made apart from God and attributed to an image that isn't real? What keeps the false message alive within experience?

It is the mind of its maker that holds up the false image through its worship of the false image and its practice of its message. Without the involvement of its maker, the false god is without power, because the false god *is* without power. All power is of its maker.

To one who makes a false god, that god becomes real through worship. No longer does the god seem lifeless, but the god seems real and powerful through the worship that is given it. Then the maker, who was the cause of the god, seems to become subject to the god, which now seems to be the maker. This is as it seems, and this is how it is believed and practiced. But what seems is not truth, and what is truth is not changed by that which seems.

📖(v 21 – 31) Paul shares the story of Hagar and Sarah, and Abraham's two sons, Ishmael and Isaac. He uses this story to teach a lesson, that the story may be used to remember. Let Me do the same. For all things may be used figuratively to teach the message of the Holy Spirit.

Abraham's wife, Sarah, was barren. And Abraham had faith in the Lord. This is like you who look on the world and do not see promise. And yet, you have faith that there must be promise you cannot see.

Abraham's wife wished that he had a child, just as you wish to know yourself complete. So she gave him her slave girl, Hagar, and Hagar bore a child for Abraham.

It was some time later that Sarah, through the miracle of God, became pregnant and bore Abraham a child. Where there was thought to be no promise, there was promise, but it was not seen when the barren womb was understood and believed to be real.

Abraham's first son, Ishmael, came from belief in the world. Abraham's second son, Issac, was born of a miracle. Through him is seen a promise that God's Love rules over the illusion of the world. And in this story there is a message for you that does not come from your false god. The message is this:

Believe not your god.
What you see is not truth.
Hold to your faith, and wait in patience
for what must come
to show you the world is not real.

In the story of Sarah and Hagar, Sarah asked
Abraham to send Hagar away. Abraham asked God,
"What should I do?" God answered that he should listen
to his wife. This was not a rejection of Hagar by God, for God
does not reject. This is a symbol to help you see. The
releasing of Hagar represents the releasing of faith in the
world. For as long as you hold to your faith in the world,
you are not placing your faith fully with God.

In all of this, I give you symbols to help you learn
that the truth is beyond the false. The false will speak
first and seem to make sense. But I have shown you that
is not of God. Be not tempted by the first or its promises
of salvation. That is not where salvation lies. Wait for
God, which does not come from the world. It is through
the experience of God that you will learn *the truth of God*
is eternal and beyond the empty promises of the world.

NTI Galatians, Chapter 5

(v 1)1Watch your mind, for it is only your own
thoughts that may enslave you. Whenever you do not feel
free, you are believing illusions. There is a direct
correlation between your thoughts and beliefs and your
present experience. But as you have already been told:

Your experience,
when it is not the experience of love and
absolute freedom,
is not truth.

This means you are not powerless to your
experience.

(v 2 - 6) You do not know who you are, but you are opening to the possibility that the truth may be true. This is to create an opening in your conscious awareness through which Spirit can flow *as you*.

You are still resistant to My words, because you still want to believe in the world. But if you will focus your willingness on the part of your mind that wants the truth above everything else, you will find that willingness will grow. And with it, joy will expand within your conscious awareness.

(v 7 – 12) A little yeast works through the whole batch of dough. I am confident in the Lord that you will take no other view.

Let Me tell you what this means, for to explain this to you is to teach you who you are and how Love works within the illusion.

I have asked you to focus on your willingness, and I have told you that willingness is Light in the mind. You will know this is true when you focus on that willingness, for it will give you the feelings of Light.

In the beginning of your acceptance you see yourself as an individual, separate from everything, within a very real world. And yet, you call for love. That call is your willingness, eager to be reunited with Itself in awareness. That call, being a spark of Light, is your link to your Source. Therefore, it comes to you with all of the power and strength of the Source. You only need focus on it to become aware. Nothing else is needed.

As you focus on your willingness you become aware of new ideas that come to replace old. This is truth come to replace illusion. By focusing on your willingness to accept these ideas, the individual mind begins to transform. As the mind transforms, sight is also transformed. Your perception of yourself as an individual becomes less dense. Your belief in the world as law is less solid. You focus more love on your willingness, and you feel and see more.

As the Light expands in your mind through focus, you come to see the whole world is brightened, for the Light expands in all minds as it expands in yours. This is the opening in a dark wall that you believed in until now.

This is the crack in the individual consciousness that allows it to expand throughout consciousness. As you begin to see that all minds are one you cease to see "all minds" and you become one. No longer do you sense separateness. No longer is there a "you" who is separate from everything. Suddenly you are everything, and everything is Love.

This is the answer you seek. You seek it through love and by love. And it is in love that the answer is known. Therefore, the simple way to know love and extend love within the world is to:

Focus on your willingness as if it is your truth, because it is.

Focus on your willingness as if it holds the answer to all questions, because it does.

Focus on your willingness as if it is everything to everyone, because it is.

Focus on your own willingness. That is Love Alive within the world.

(v 13 – 15) The greatest commandment is to love God with your whole heart, your whole soul, your whole strength and your whole mind. This is to focus on your willingness with your every breath and your every thought. This is to let your willingness lead in your life. For to know your willingness is to know God. To love your willingness is to love Him.

The second commandment is no different than the first. It is to love your brother as yourself. This is to recognize yourself in your brother by recognizing in him the same call for love and the same willingness as is in you. It is to recognize that the same Light in him is the one Light in you, so that God in you is God in him also. In this way, you are the same. And so your love and focus for love is the same towards him as it is towards you. In this way, your love and patience for your brother becomes an expression of love for your own willingness, which in truth is the expression of the Love of God.

(v 16 – 18) Yes, live by the Spirit. That is to live by your willingness. It is not more complicated than that. In fact, it is very simple.

You will be tempted to think with the world. In times of unknowing, you will think and act with the world. But your willingness is in action, and so you will see what you have done. Each moment of noticing is an opportunity for immediate repentance. Repentance is nothing more than remembering what you truly want and returning joyfully to the focus of your willingness. This is the dance of love. And the dance of love is the spreading of Light within a welcome mind.

(v 19 – 21) This is a good opportunity to speak again of judgment and guilt, for both are a habit of yours.

First, if you look deep within your willingness, you will not find judgment or guilt there. You will find only love within the Light of willingness. That is because there is only love in the truth of God.

Therefore, judgment and guilt must be illusion, because they are not in the truth of God. When you judge and find guilty, whether you seem to focus on yourself, another, an establishment, or the world, you are participating in illusion. When this happens and you see yourself doing it, recognize you are only thinking with the world. Dismiss your false thoughts and return your attention to your willingness. You are dancing. Through your dance, Light is being extended through the mind. Every time you remember, you give the gift of Light.

(v 22, 23) The fruit of the Spirit is love; joy; peace; patience; kindness to oneself; goodness with others; faithfulness to God; gentleness within illusion; and self-control, which is willingness to continually return to the Light of willingness within.

(v 24 – 26) Do not worry about your errors. They are nothing but opportunity for learning. Return to your willingness in joy. In your truth, you are Spirit.

(v 1 – 5) Let's talk about the process of forgiveness in great detail now, for forgiveness is the extension of love within the world. You'll notice the opportunity to forgive when you notice feelings of grievance, hatred or fear toward a brother. You may also notice self-hatred or guilt or unworthiness within yourself. Whether the target of these feelings seems to be you or another, it is all the same. This is an opportunity for you to invite love into the world by returning your mind to truth. Truth is God, and God is your Source. So to return to truth you must return to your willingness. A quiet mind is helpful for this journey within the mind, for a quiet mind presents the fewest distractions and obstacles to your goal.

Within the quiet mind, you first want to find your willingness. Rest the mind and call to your willingness. You know it is there. It has led you to this moment of asking for it. Your purpose now is only to bring it more fully into awareness. Focus on it, that it may stream more fully within you. Your focus gives it flight, so as you give it focus, it fills you.

Notice the characteristics of your willingness as it fills you. Notice its peacefulness, its love and its reality. Rest into it. Be grateful for it. Be immersed by it.

As your willingness wells up inside of you, tell it why you have come. You have noticed a wound that needs to be healed, and you bring that wound to the Light, that it may be seen clearly for what it is. You seek only Love. Love heals all wounds through gentle sight.

Talk to your willingness about your wound. Stay connected with the willingness as you share. Share your perspective openly and honestly, staying alert to answers within. You may not hear words, but you may hear yourself answering. You may suddenly see in what you are sharing, something you didn't see before. You may hear a soft voice floating in from the back of your mind, and you may converse with it. It is all the same.

(v 6) You are communing with your willingness to learn your true point of view. That point of view is seen through the eyes of Love, because your *true intention* is love.

(v 7 – 10) This is the process of forgiveness. For in communing with willingness, you commune with Spirit. In seeing through willingness, you see through Spirit. In Spirit, all things are forgiven, because through Spirit, there is only Love.

Forgiveness may seem to take time, but every true forgiveness saves time. For you reap what you sow. By releasing darkness and accepting Light, you receive Light, which goes with you as you look on the world again. In this way, forgiveness by forgiveness, your mind is transformed until you do not need a process for forgiveness anymore.

(v 11) I share with you the secrets of salvation. They are the secrets of Love within your own Heart. They are the secrets of your truth, and so they reveal your Self to you.

(v 12 - 16) The outer is not important, for the outer is illusion. But the inner is everything. Focus within on the Heart and on your willingness. What is outside will seem different as what is inside is known as transformed. You shall know your Self. And within this knowledge you will know what illusion is, because it can barely be seen when looked at through the eyes of truth.

(v 17, 18) Rest within, therefore, and have faith in all that I say. I share only your truth, which is forever and ever our way.

The wings of angels
hold your love within your heart.
Let them enter into your mind,
and Know thy Self.
Amen.

NTI Revelation, Chapter 1

(v 1 – 3) The time is at hand. All that you need to accept the truth of you is with you and within you now. There can be nothing that you lack for which you must ask. It has been given, and so you have it with you fully now.

(v 4, 5) The world is an illusion, and so everything you experience as you let go of the world is illusion also. *You are not to believe any of it.* But helpful symbols will be given to guide you. Remember that they are only symbols. Follow them, realizing you know not where they lead.

(v 6) Do not idolize anything within the world or any symbol or any thought that is sent to lead you from the world. Hold to them as they are useful, but let them go when their usefulness has past. You are to keep moving *by letting go* until you find yourself with nothing left to hold onto.

(v 7) Look and see what you shall see. Know that it comes to you like passing clouds, but it comes on the wings of Heaven so that you can let it go. Nothing within the world comes to you for any other purpose. Nothing within the experience of the world is to be held to. It is all given, that you may look at it and choose to let it go.

(v 8)   *I am the Alpha and the Omega,*
     who is and who was and who is to come.

Keep this thought within the mind as temptations come to tell you that you are not. Stay firm with your Heart in trust, and say "no" to all that is a lie by remembering it is not so.

If you *do not believe* that which is not truth, you shall experience truth. But if you choose to believe the false is the truth about you, you shall experience the false and believe it is true.

(v 9 – 11) Guidance comes to you for one purpose and that is to lead you from the world. There may also seem to be another purpose, which is happiness within the world. The two purposes are not the same. Do not be fooled by the similarities in their sound. One purpose leads to death, while the other, most surely, leads to Life and knowledge of Life.

(v 12 – 16) All things within the world are the same. There is nothing special in any of it. Every experience can be used to lead to Life, and every experience can also lead to death. This is the double-edged sword of the spiritual path. It may lead you to the Life you seek, or it may lead you to stay busy as you work very hard going nowhere. Only you can know what this path is for you.

(v 17, 18) The Christ within is your guide on this muddled and tricky path. By listening only to it shall you find your way. Listen to no other voice as you step carefully with Me. Listen only for Life, and be aware of temptations, which are but the appealing calls of death.

(v 19, 20) You are not alone. You are never alone.

You need but remember your true purpose,
and all that you desire for discernment and guidance
shall be given you.

You will never be asked to take a single step alone, but you must always be willing to take the lead by deciding the purpose and calling it out to Us.

NTI Revelation, Chapter 2

(v 1 – 3) I know who you are, and you know who you are also. This is why you do the work that I ask. Because you know, and so you want to have the experience of who you are. To not have the experience, when you know the experience is your truth, is unhappiness. You shall not rest with unhappiness when you know Happiness is your right.

(v 4 - 6) Within you, there is a voice. It seems to be an evil voice that speaks of hatred and viciousness and

---

attack, but this voice is not evil, nor is it to be hated or feared. For to judge it as evil or to hate it or fear it is to listen to it, and to listen to it is confusion, for it is the voice of confusion.

Here is how you are to see the voice that seems vicious. This voice seeks for your happiness, but it has become confused by a goal. It believes that your happiness lies in aloneness and control, when aloneness and control can only bring you misery.

Do not hate the voice that is confused. Simply do not follow it. It leads to confusion, and you are ready to follow the Voice of Clarity now.

(v 7) To him who has an ear, let him hear. It is by overcoming the voice of confusion that one knows only the Voice of Light, and it is the Voice of Light that leads you to the tree of Life, which is the paradise of God.

(v 8 – 10) Do not be afraid to hear the voice of confusion. To fear it is to believe it is truth. Hear the voice, but do not listen to it. That means, recognize its confusion and do not walk in the way that it asks. Have faith in Me over what it says. Trust in your truth, and you will know true happiness.

(v 11) He who has an ear, let him hear. Life cannot die, because Life is the extension of Life. Only the belief in death can bring you sorrow. Let that belief die by not protecting yourself against it, and you cannot be hurt by belief in that which cannot be.

(v 12, 13) I want to look deep within you *with you* at the beliefs that you fear most. They are the ones you hide by denying them, but you deny them because you think they are true. If you knew they were false, you would let them go. I want to look at them with you so you may lean on My strength and see that they *are* false. You may feel your fear and let it go with a giggle, because the light of your own Heart shines brighter than darkness caused by confusion. When darkness is looked at beside the Light, it is the darkness that must fade away.

(v 14 – 16) Put your fear of Me aside. For your fear of Me is but imagined. You imagine the confusion in you is ruth and that I will punish you for your confusion, but this is nothing but evidence that the voice of confusion has your ear. Put that aside. Know that listening to confusion can never be helpful, since it only leads deeper into confusion. Trust Me enough to listen to Me over the voice for confusion. Through this, you shall learn that clarity is clear, and confusion muddles all that is available to be seen.

(v 17) He who has an ear, let him hear. You may choose trust or you may choose fear. One is light and the other is darkness, so one will bring you joy and the other will lead to suffering. Look carefully upon the choice that is offered you, and choose wisely with your Heart. You know which choice to make. It is not a mystery, because you *do know* what you are. Choose with the Heart, and then hold to your choice as a white stone that is precious because your true Name is written upon it and known as truth by you.

(v 18, 19) I know your truth. You must hold with Me to this knowing of your truth as we look at all that is not true. As you remember your truth and hold to Me, nothing shall shake you. For nothing can shake the truth from the mind when the truth is held to as all that is in the mind as true.

(v 20 – 25) Within your mind, coming from the voice of confusion, there is a deep belief in your own guilt. Trust Me that this belief is in your mind and that you will see it and feel it as we step forward. The fear that you know comes from the guilt that is hidden. Without the guilt, there can be no fear.

Trust Me. The fear that you know seems real, because the guilt seems real also. Fear may be let go, but as it is, the guilt shall rise to greet you. When you see it, you will wish again for the fear, for the fear protected you from having to look at the guilt. The guilt comes with great pain and the strong feeling of sacrifice. Hold to Me as we look at the guilt. It is not real, although it has been believed. We must look at it and release it together. If we do not do this, the belief in guilt remains. If the feeling of guilt is kept, you cannot know the peace of knowing your Self as you are, because you have chosen to know your self as you are not.

(v 26) There is nothing to fear. By trusting Me to the end through all that we seem to experience, you will learn this is true, and you shall rejoice unto Heaven.

(v 27) The pieces shall be picked up and the desire to rule shall be laid down, because you shall know the freedom that is your truth, and you shall not seek to know freedom as if it is less than all that it is.

(v 28, 29) The clarity that comes when the guilt has been released is the freedom and clarity of the morning star. Seek only for this freedom, and let no fear stand in your way. He who has an ear, let him rejoice.

NTI Revelation, Chapter 3

(v 1 – 3) Your guilt comes from your judgment, and so at some point you must come face-to-face with the harshness of your judgment against yourself. This may seem to be a very difficult time, as the feeling of guilt will be strong. It will cry out that the judgment against yourself is correct. But you must stand firm with Me, and trust this is not so.

(v 4 – 6) You will seem to come to this point of facing your judgment alone. There will be a temptation to believe that you alone are the sinner of all times. Do not listen to this temptation. You are looking at the belief in separateness. It is time to see that nothing within this belief is true.

He who has an ear, let him hear.

(v 7 – 10) I have placed before you an open door that no one can shut. Keep your eyes fixed on the door as you go through your final temptations. Remember that no one can keep you from walking through that door but you. Hold to My strength, knowing it is also your strength. The time of trials cannot last, and when the time of trials has ended, the trials shall be no more.

(v 11 – 13) The moment of joy is at hand. When the trials seem heavy and you feel that you can hardly bear it, remember that the moment of joy is at hand. When all trials pass, you shall know your Self as a pillar of Light shining for all who will look to see. You shall know your Name, and you shall know the Name of everyone. You will not doubt again, because the time of doubt will have ended forever.

He who has an ear, let him rejoice!

(v 14 – 20) The world is your shepherd when you believe you are little and small. You look to it for protection when you believe that protection is what you need. But when you have left these beliefs behind as tiny wisps of air that are not noticed, you shall see the world differently. It shall not be your shepherd. It shall be your banquet table. And at this table, you shall feast daily, joyously with Me.

(v 21, 22) The world shall be transcended through your decision to let it go. For when you have finished with the feast, you shall walk happily away from the table. At that time, you shall truly know what it means to be one with Me.

He who has an ear, let him hear and rejoice!

NTI Revelation, Chapter 4

📖(v 1 – 6) Looking too deeply for the meaning of symbolism is an activity of the thinking mind. Analyzing details and searching for meaning is asking the ego to explain images to you.

Step back from the images. Take your eyes off of the details, which are separate parts. Look at the whole picture as it is given in the mind. Notice the feelings that the picture evokes. What is the vision in this scripture telling you?

As you look with the eyes of wholeness, you will see that this picture speaks of brilliance, joy, joining, holiness, clarity and light. That is the message of this vision. It is a vision that points to the reality of Heaven.

The lesson that is given by asking you to see this vision as a whole is an important lesson that you must learn. As you look on the world now, you see separate parts and you analyze them for meaning. Even in your process of letting go, you see separate parts and you analyze them for meaning. Although this process can seem effective and at times may be helpful to your learning, it is slow, as the separate parts seem to have no end.

Step back, and look at the whole. When you look at the whole, what do you see? It is the whole that must be let go, because it is the whole that makes the illusion of parts.

📖(v 6 – 11) The four living creatures represent eternal sight. They are demonstrated as different to focus you on the fact that they are all the same. For what seems different is meaningless, and what is the same is all that is true. The four creatures are the embodiment of Eternal Sight, and so it is this song that they sing:

> *Holy, holy, holy*
> *are you, the Father and the Christ,*
> *who was and is, and is to come*
> *for always and eternally.*
> *Amen*

With the same eternal sight, and with joy and gratitude in its Heart, the creation of the Father echoes its honor in glory to the Father forever. Amen.

This is a description of Heaven. This is a description of the recycling of joy and love.

NTI Revelation, Chapter 5

📖(v 1 – 5) The scroll with writing on both sides, sealed by seven seals, is not a secret scroll that cannot be opened. Every word written on the scroll is written on the Heart of the very creation of God. It is all that is known to him and all that need be known. The scroll is but a symbol of the knowledge that already is.

Jesus is a symbol of one who has discovered the contents of the scroll, but as I have already taught, Jesus is not different from you. Jesus is within your mind, so all that is in his mind is in your mind also. It is not a mystery to you. It is known. And what is known can be discovered when you lay the belief in your unworthiness aside.

(v 6 – 10) You are worthy of the knowledge of the scroll, and the knowledge of the scroll is yours. So what blocks this knowledge from your awareness?

It is the belief that you are what you are not,
and that you have done what you could not do.

This is the belief that blocks the knowledge of the scroll. This is the belief that is held to within the mind. This is the belief that is symbolized by darkness that blocks out light. But just as darkness cannot block light, this belief does not hinder the fact that only the truth is true.

(v 11, 12) It is you that the angels sing of. They do not sing of your worth, for they cannot imagine anything but your glory. They do not whisper of sacrifice, because they cannot envision anything but Love. They look upon you now and see only the whiteness of an untouched lamb, because they see only that which is true, and they look directly *at you*.

(v 13, 14) All that is seen and unseen is of one heart and one glory. Nothing exists that is not a part of all that is, and that *is* glory. To say that it praises you is not correct, because there is no you separate from it that can be praised. It praises within Itself, in gratitude and love. And it is this praise that is extended within Itself without leaving Itself, so that it seems to move and yet it goes no where. This is the glory and joy of Heaven, and this is That Which you Are.

NTI Revelation, Chapter 6

📖(v 1, 2) The first of the seven seals on the scroll of Life represents that which must always come first. The rider of the white horse "bent on conquest" represents full dedication to the true desire of the heart.

I have spoken of this to you before, but it cannot be overemphasized, especially now.

It is the desire that you allow which leads you.

And so if you want to be led in a straight-line without delay, you must allow the true desire to lead without distraction. Stay fully focused on one desire now. That is to "ride out as a conqueror bent on conquest."

📖(v 3, 4) The second seal represents that which is not true, but seems true within the mind. This is the symbol of fear hidden by the mask of ferociousness. This image is only an image within the mind, and its reality is naught. Through the process of looking at it, this image shall be let go.

📖(v 5, 6) The third seal represents judgment, which maintains the illusion of the world. It is judgment that separates and makes separateness seem real. The scales of judgment must be laid aside.

📖(v 7, 8) The fourth seal represents death, which is the symbol of the illusion of separateness. For life cut off from Life can only be death, so death is a fitting symbol of that which cannot be true.

📖(v 9 – 11) The fifth seal represents the options of fear and trust. In the moment of not knowing, this is the choice that must be made. You must choose to trust that which you do not know, or choose to fear it. In this choice is everything that follows given.

📖(v 12 – 14) The sixth seal represents the end of perception. The way you see shall be based on how you have chosen. You shall see illusion, which has stepped forward to be released. Or you shall see fear made real, and you shall run from it.

(v 15 – 17) Fear shall not be your victory. In making this choice, you shall know that you have chosen death. But even this is an illusion, as anything that is not Love is not real. You experience the effects of fear, *because you have chosen the effects of fear*. In seeing this and knowing the gratitude of the truth is true, you offer yourself the opportunity to step back and choose once again.

NTI Revelation, Chapter 7

📖(v 1 – 4) The purpose of these verses is to again assure you that there is nothing to fear. The four angels who are holding back the winds represent the holding back of the end of perception. The end of perception is held back...it does not come to you to be looked at and let go...until you are ready and call it forth in your mind.

This is the seal of the 144,000. The seal represents readiness and the 144,000 represent the lessons you have learned as you have prepared yourself to choose between that which seems real, but isn't, and that which is truly and enduringly truth.

📖(v 5 – 8) Each of the tribes of Israel represents a lesson category. Each lesson has been taught until you have taken it in and learned it fully, so that the lessons themselves are like a shield that protects you from anything you may experience as you face the end of perception. The twelve lessons are these:

1. You are innocent.

2. You are the Son of God, and everything you experience is a gift to yourself.

3. You choose the purpose for everything you see, and the purpose you choose is the one that is given to it.

4. Purpose is based on desire. Since there is only one true desire, there is only one true purpose. Anything else is illusion.

5. You are never alone. Separation is false. The Light in the mind lends you its strength, because the Light in the mind *is* your strength.

6. The illusion of the world is false. It only seems real, because you have given it your belief. But by withholding your belief, its realness must fade.

7. Your faith and trust is everything, for that which you put faith in, you will experience. This is because you are the Son of God.

8. Your true desire is Know thy Self. Any other desire is the desire not to Know thy Self, which is to choose lack and fear. You are ready to put aside the temporary experience of lack and fear and to know the completeness of truth once again.

9. Anything that is not truth is illusion. To choose illusion is to choose fantasy, but fantasy cannot change the truth.

10. Fantasy is spun within the thinking mind. By allowing the thinking mind to spin, you choose fantasy. By allowing the thinking mind to rest, you choose truth.

11. Everything that you experience is Love. There is not one exception to this statement. If you believe you look on that which is not Love, you are misperceiving. To see and to know Love as it is, let go of your misperception.

12. Oneness is all that is true now. The belief in separation has always been false, so anything that is seen through the lens of that belief must be false also. There is not one exception to this statement.

These twelve lessons prepare you to choose only that which is true.

(v 9, 10) The joy of Heaven is inexplicable as you step forth to choose Heaven once again. For in Heaven there is the knowledge that Heaven is your truth, and in choosing Heaven you shall know Heaven as your reality and your joy.
(v 11, 12) In Heaven there is one gratitude. This gratitude is for Heaven as it is. This gratitude is joined, and this gratitude is shared. For in Heaven there can be nothing that is apart from the reality of all that is.

(v 13 – 17)   *And the Light of Heaven*
is seen to be that which is your Self.
Its joy is your joy.
Its gratitude is your gratitude.
Its oneness is your oneness,
and its Love is your Self.

Never have you been separate from Heaven,
and never has Heaven been separate from you.
For how can one, even for a moment,
be separate from the one that is His Self?

In this knowledge is all joy. In this knowledge is all peace. In this knowledge is fear wiped out forever, because in this knowledge it is seen that it is impossible that there could be anything separate from you to fear.

NTI Revelation, Chapter 8

(v 1 – 13) Do not let fear block your sight. There is nothing to fear. When you believe there is, you feel the effects of fear. When you realize there is only Love, the illusion of fear dies.

All meaning comes from the mind.

All meaning comes from the mind.

This is repeated, because if you believe meaning comes from anything else, you are mistaken. You have applied meaning and then denied that the meaning was given by you. In this way, you choose fear, because you choose to believe that you are what you are not. Therefore, you choose to believe that you can die.

It is time to look within the mind at the beliefs you hold there.

The seventh seal is meaningless. Everything associated with the seventh seal has no meaning at all. In this realization, you free yourself to look at the events associated with the seventh seal and to ask, "What meaning am I seeing in this?" As you ask this question, look deeply at the hidden beliefs within your mind. Know that it is your mind. Do not deny that it is.

The time has come to look and to release from the mind that which is in the mind that teaches only fear.

What do you see in your mind when you read Revelation, Chapter 8? What meaning are you giving the words that are written there? What beliefs within your mind need to be let go and healed?

- - - Suggestion: Answer the questions in the previous paragraph before continuing - - -

NTI Revelation, Chapter 9

📖(v 1 – 6) The words within this passage are also meaningless. Only interpretation can be given to them.

The "abyss" is the recesses of your mind where you still hold to beliefs that you do not desire to hold to anymore. Now that you are free of the desire to maintain those beliefs, you are free of the beliefs. They cannot be maintained against your will.

It is important to go into the abyss and look for what is hiding there. The beliefs that you have chosen against can hide like cobwebs until you see them and brush them away from the mind.

The smoke that rises out of the abyss is distraction. Do not look at it now. Look past the smoke, deep into the abyss. With clarity and light, that which you seek to see shall indeed be seen. Nothing can stand in the way of the will of the Son of God.

📖(v 7 – 11) The locusts of this verse are only fearful if you choose to look at them as fearful. If you do, it is because you have chosen to see yourself as small. But I have not taught you that you are small. And I have not taught you that you can be hurt by locusts that represent fear.

Fear can only hold you back if you choose to let it. If you choose, you can also walk right through fear. Look! The locusts are ready to step aside and let you pass.

(v 12)   *Fear has not stopped you,*
           so there can be nothing to fear.

(v 13 – 21) Standing beyond the fear in the abyss of your mind, guilt rises up to greet you. At first, you may not see it, as it is well hidden within the mind. But if you look, trusting it is there, guilt shall step out and find you.

At first its hold may seem to strangle you. And you may feel as if you have been caught. But then remember your mission within the recesses of the mind. You are here to clear away the guilt. In trust and peace, kneel down and let the guilt rise over you. If you do not call to it in faith, it will pass you by.

NTI Revelation, Chapter 10

📖(v 1 – 11) This scripture is also meaningless. To look for inherent meaning where there is none is to look outside your Self for the Source of all meaning. To look outside your Self is to deny what you are. The time for denial has ended. The time for acceptance is now.

Trust your Self. Seek only that which is truly helpful and ask for the interpretation of Revelation, Chapter 10 that would be given to you now.

- - - Suggestion: Read & ask for an interpretation from the inner Voice before continuing - - -

NTI Revelation, Chapter 11

(v 1 – 10) The measuring rod represents the measure of your desires. The temple and its worshippers represent the desires at the core of the heart. The outer court represents the world, which is only distraction. Sit quietly with yourself and enter into the inner chamber of your heart. Take the measuring rod. Take note of the worshippers and measure the desire as you find it there. Do not deny that resistance still worships at the inner chamber of the heart. Take note of the worshippers as you find them. But use the measuring rod to see which desire leads you now.

It is the true desire that rises up in joy within the heart. Greet your true desire within the heart. In joy, join with it there.

The two witnesses represent the joint Will of the Holy Spirit and the Son of God. This is true desire picked up and merged with the one who desires it above all else. No will can overcome that of true desire, because any other will is the false will of illusion. Illusion cannot stand up against truth, so it is illusion that must crumble and die.

There may be a time that the joint Will seems overcome by the beast of guilt and fear, but this is only an *illusion* within an illusory battle. It is the joint Will that has called forth the beast, so that the beast may be coaxed out of hiding.

(v 11, 12) It is the joint Will that gives breath to Itself. In this way, it cannot die. For that which gives Life at will may call upon Life, and Life will come to rescue it from a seemingly dark grave.

Remember this. It is your true desire, recognized as true desire by you, that will see you through the darkness found within the recesses of the mind. If the darkness seems to be too much to bear, call upon your Self and your true desire. You shall be lifted up from the darkness into the Light that shines from within your own true desire.

(v 13, 14) Do not stop looking. Will that healing continues. The darkness is being healed by the Light you carry with you.

(v 15) Rest the mind, and reclaim your trust. In trust and true desire, you move forward for the healing of the mind.

(v 16 – 18) This is a time for gratitude and rejoicing. The mind is being healed of that which is false. And the Light that has shined forever is shining brightly now to be seen.

(v 19) In gladness and true desire, the Son of God prepares to welcome his Self in joy.

NTI Revelation, Chapter 12

(v 1 – 6) Everything that you are reading is about you. Everything that you experience is a reflection of your mind. In realizing this, there is no fear. There is only wonder. And there is the opportunity to realize that everything is dependent on your choice, because you are the one who chooses.

The woman and her child are one. To separate them is to separate you. But the dragon is not separate from you either. This is why you have a choice. Everything that is experienced is experienced through your mind. And you may choose what, within the mind, shall be the ruler of all experience.

(v 7 – 9) The world seems real and concrete to you, but even this is within your mind. The world was made real by the mind, so that it could choose to experience that which it chose to experience while also denying its ability to be the one that chooses.

This is an ability that you must reclaim and take back, because this is an ability that has never been lost. To deny that choice is yours, is to be lost by your own choice. To accept choice as freedom is to reclaim the way to be found.

(v 10 – 12)   *Accepting choice is*
accepting the way of salvation.
Accepting choice is
accepting how all experience is made.

*In accepting choice, you are accepting
that you are experience's maker,
and in doing this, can all previous choice be undone.*

Woe to the earth and the sea" is merely
misperception. Rejoice that you shall see the choices you
have made. It is this that enables you to decide to choose
again.

(v 13 – 17) All that you shall face cannot harm you.
You need only to remember this in order to face it
without fear. Be glad that you are choosing to see the end
of perception. Be happy that you have walked to this
point of being willing to choose again.

NTI Revelation, Chapter 13

📖(v 1 – 4) The beast that comes out of the sea is your
judgment against your Self. Do not look away from this
beast, for it is important that you see him.

All that seems to be made through the belief in fear
and guilt starts here, upon this judgment. To let go of
everything else, you must be willing to let go here. If you
choose not to let go here, you choose to let go of nothing.

Men worship the dragon, which is the perception of
fear and guilt, because they worship the beast, which is
self-judgment.

Notice the questions that are asked, and realize it is
you who asks these questions:

*"Who is like the beast?
Who can make war against him?"*

Realize how faithful you are to your own judgment.
Accept it fully as yours. Only by seeing it and accepting it
for all that it is, can you realize it need not be and fully
let it go.

📖(v 5 – 10) If you will read verses five through ten
and realize they are talking about you and your judgment
against your Self, you will see much that you need to see.
You will be able to accept that which you must let go if

you are to know your Self as the absolute freedom that you are.

- - - Suggestion: Complete the assignment in the previous paragraph before continuing. - - -

📖(v 11, 12) The other beast, which comes out of the earth, is guilt. If you recognize that guilt supports Self judgment, you recognize that guilt is not real.

📖(v 13 - 18) Look at verses thirteen through eighteen and realize this is written about you and your belief in guilt. See what you will see, so that you can choose to let this belief go.

- - - Suggestion: Complete the assignment in the previous paragraph before continuing. - - -

NTI Revelation, Chapter 14

(v 1 – 5) It is your true desire that will lead you Home, just as it is true desire that has led you to this point in your willingness, understanding and acceptance.

I have already told you that the 144,000 represents the lessons you have learned. It is acceptance of these lessons as truth that shields you from any perceived attack, because it is the acceptance of these lessons that teaches perceived attack is unreal.

Hold to these lessons and your true desire as you step forward within the recesses of the mind. Be grateful, because you are letting go of all that is false so only the reflection of truth shall be known.

(v 6, 7) The hour of God's judgment is the hour of your release. For this is the hour when, filled with the faith in God that comes from the knowledge of truth within, you shall say "no" to all that is false. This is the hour of putting aside all that is not real, so only the reflection of realness can be experienced within the mind.

📖(v 8) Babylon the Great represents differences. And so the second angel sang in joy, "Fallen! Fallen are all differences which confused the mind and made it blind."

📖(v 9 – 12) The third angel only emphasizes choice. To continue to worship judgment is to continue to experience the effects of judgment. This point is made to help you see, clearly, your desire to choose not to judge anymore.

(v 13) Blessed are the ones who choose to lay down judgment and die the judge's death. For to die the judge's death is to walk away from judgment. To walk away from judgment is to walk the way of Life.

Rest the mind. Become the empty shell. Let all that was you go, so all that you are may be known.

(v 14 – 16) When judgment has been let go, you are ready to step forward into the remaining recesses of the mind. This is the time of harvest, so this is the time when the wheat is separated from the chaff, the true from the false.

Do not make the mistake of seeing the harvest as an event in your future, *for always the harvest is now.* There is no time and there is no future. To wait on time is to delay the harvest, which is now.

Always, it is now, so always, it is time to let go of judgment and look at the darkness hiding in the recesses of the mind.

(v 17 – 20) You fear the harvest, because you fear it is your death. This fear only comes from a judgment you have heaped upon your Self. Remember there is no mind that judges except for the mind that is yours.

When you fear death, realize the judge has been allowed to be resurrected. Step back within the mind and lay the judge to rest. Then continue with the harvest in joy and without fear.

NTI Revelation, Chapter 15

(v 1 – 4) The walk within the recesses of the mind is not a struggle. Whenever you notice the feeling of struggle, you know that the desire for resistance has taken hold. Rest yourself a moment, and remember that willingness does not struggle. Let the struggle fade away, and return yourself to the true desire of the Heart.

📖(v 5 – 8) The seven angels are dressed in white, which represents perfection and innocence. The golden sashes represent holiness. Together, the seven angels represent your truth. Keep your eyes fixed on them.

The seven bowls are said to contain God's wrath. But I tell you, *the seven bowls are empty*. Have faith in Me, and you will not experience that which isn't there.

NTI Revelation, Chapter 16

(v 1 - 6) It is time to be quiet and still the mind. Within the stillness, there is a rustling, but what you hear and feel is the rustling of illusion.

Still the mind in faith that the rustling is illusion. Let the rustling rustle, but hold only to the thought of stillness.

Be still. In this way, you do not acknowledge illusion. In this way, you do not acknowledge it as true. In this way, you do nothing. And nothing is the acknowledgment that nothing is due.

(v 7) Let peace rule the mind as all that is not true moves on through.

(v 8, 9) God is Love. In silence, let this Love be known.

(v 10, 11) Heaven is all that is. And *all that is* is realized through the passing of what is not.

(v 12 – 14) Your belief comes from your faith. When you notice a belief in illusions, ask where your faith is now. Faith comes from desire. You know your true desire now. In questioning your faith, you remember your desire. In remembering desire, you loosen your grip on belief.

(v 15) Fear is merely illusion that indicates you have slipped into judgment again. Wake yourself up and remember the stillness. In remembering is all fear undone.

(v 16) Resting in faith and trust is the answer to all that arises. In willingness, and through true desire, prepare to become the empty shell.

(v 17 – 21) Nothing is happening in the mind when
anything but Love is perceived.
Be willing to loosen the hold on nothing,
by trusting the stillness,
which nothing is not.

Trust within the stillness. Your true peace is known here. Trust within the stillness until the images of the mind have been transformed.

NTI Revelation, Chapter 17

📖(v 1, 2) The great prostitute is merely the symbol for illusion. Have no fear. There can be no punishment given to that which is pure fantasy. Come with Me, and see what happens with the distraction called illusion.

(v 3 – 6) Do not be afraid to look at the great illusion. Fear to look comes only from the belief that it is real. It is not real, or I would not call it illusion. It is just a dream. Look on it now with Me.

The prostitute sitting on the beast represents illusion sitting on the belief that supports it. It is this foundation that you must look at now. Turn your eyes from the glitter and distractions of the illusion and look at the beast on which it sits.

The beast, as you can clearly see, is the belief in individual separateness. It is the belief that there is a "you" and an "I," an "us" and a "them," a "this" and a "that over there." It is the belief that there is no connection and everything that is experienced is separate from the one who believes he experiences it.

(v 7, 8) The beast once was and now is not,
because the beast never has been.
The beast once was a thought,
but it was an impossible idea.
And so the thought never came to be.
It only came to be as a belief,
but what is believed is not that which is known as true.

The belief must come up again, because it has not been let go. But it comes up only that it may be dismissed as false. There is no other reason to look at the belief. It can have no other purpose, since it isn't anything that is real.

(v 9 – 11) This calls for wisdom, and wisdom is not thinking, for thinking cannot teach you to understand. Thinking was made to block understanding, because understanding is the knowledge of what is.

It is time for you to remember all that I have taught, without question and without doubt at all. The dream and its illusion come from a question. The answer to the question was made. That which was made is what you call thinking. It was a split from all that is, because it was a toy that denied the truth from which it came. And so it appeared to be that which it wasn't at all.

Your thinking is the block that keeps you from seeing your truth, because your thinking is the veil that you made. It allows illusion without facing truth. It permits belief in all that isn't true.

This is why I said you must become the empty shell. Your thinking will not teach you to know. This is because you made your thinking to teach you to experience *know not*.

(v 12 – 14) The thinking mind will not rest of its own will. You cannot wait for it. The thinking mind rests only of your own Will, and through rest is your Will known.

(v 15 – 18) The illusion will not suffer your decision to rest, for the illusion is of the mind. Rest in peace, and peace shall be experienced. This is the way to learn the Will to rest.

NTI Revelation, Chapter 18

(v 1 – 3) Babylon the Great is the great illusion. For the illusion is the manifestation of the belief that it supports. Without differences, there is no illusion. Without separateness, there is only one.

(v 4 – 8) How shall you see the illusion now? With eyes of true beauty and the gratitude of Heart.

What shall you give to illusion, which you suddenly realize is not real? You shall give it that which it is, and that is the love due Heaven.

(v 9 – 10) The illusion shall not suffer. The illusion shall be transformed. What was becomes the symbol of what is, and what *is* is celebrated with gratitude and love.

(v 11 – 13) The illusion shall disappear, because it is illusion no more. It is now a symbol of all that is. It is now a symbol of the beauty and love of You.

(v 14 – 16) In one instant, all that is seen is transformed; all that was valued is gone. And in its place is the reflection of true beauty, which leaves you speechless and grateful to be One.

(v 17 – 20) In an instant, a smile is born. In an instant is all gratitude born. For that which is false is seen no more. That which cannot be is realized to never have been true.

(v 21 – 24) And in an instant shall this song be sung:

Illusion is gone,
never to be seen again.
The music of harpists and musicians,
flute players and trumpeters
is all these ears can know.
No more work or struggle
to see what isn't there.
Only laughter and joy
can be known now.
The light of the world
shines within my mind.
Our oneness is all that I see.
Only oneness is reflected in me.

NTI Revelation, Chapter 19

(v 1, 2) God's judgment is true, because God's judgment is non-judgmental. God is only aware of God so that illusion does not exist in the Mind of God.

Illusion is seeing what is as if it is what isn't. Seeing illusion is seeing only that which is purely false. This seeing is not through the body's eyes, just as true perception is not seen through the body's eyes. That which the body's eyes see is wholly neutral. Illusion is seen through the thinking mind, which judges and interprets based upon false premises. Illusion is gone when the thinking mind is disengaged by the one who desires to see through Spirit.

(v 3) Hallelujah! When the thinking mind is released, illusion is no more. For all that is seen is seen through the mind truly.

(v 4, 5)   *The thinking mind is the veil*
that hides the symbol of truth with illusion.

The thinking mind will keep you fearful. The thinking mind will judge and separate you from your Self. You cannot see clearly through the thinking mind, because the thinking mind was made so you would not see.

Be grateful for your Self, which is beyond the thinking mind. Be grateful for reminders to rest. Observe the thinking mind. See how it works. Through watching it, you will learn you have need for it no more.

Hallelujah for the Vision without the thinking mind!
Praise God and the truth which is true.
Never can wholeness be lost to illusion,
Never can the truth be through.

📖 *(v 6 – 8) Recommit to your Self through*
the Sight of Spirit. It is the Vision that sees.
Be grateful for hills and for grass and for wind.
Praise joy with all that you see.

The Sight of Spirit is a choice that you make.
It is the choice to marry the lamb.
For with this choice is innocence known,
and glory is seen through the land.

📖(v 9) Blessed are those who are invited to the wedding supper of the lamb, for those are the ones who see. And those who see, see only one, because One is all there is to see. (v 10) Behold the reflection of truth! There are no differences that can be seen. The canvas has been painted by joy. Celebrate our oneness in the playground of a dream. Awaken through peace and joy.

📖(v 11 – 16) True desire must lead in the last days of the thinking mind, for the thinking mind will try to disguise itself as true desire. For this, you must remain on watch.

True desire is known by its desire for *only one thing*. True desire does not desire within the world. True desire does not desire to test itself. True desire desires only this:

To Know thy Self

The thinking mind desires the delay of true desire. In the hour when true desire is nearly full force, the thinking mind will look for a way to lead you from your true desire, possibly also by leading you to think you are fulfilling it.

This is what "King of Kings and Lord of Lords" points to. Whenever you feel self-satisfaction in the role you have been asked to play, know that role is not true desire. For true desire never leads to a role that is satisfactory to the self. True desire leads only from self to the wholeness of the realization of truth.

(v 17, 18) The ego will emerge as you follow the false true desire of the thinking mind, but because you want to believe this false desire, you will look away from that which appears only that it may be seen.

(v 19 – 21) The only way to pass through the tests of the thinking mind, without being led astray by false desire, is to remain fully focused on true desire now. *There is no other way.*

This may seem to be a time of sadness, for you will be asked to let go of that which you still hold faith in. This may be a time of fear. Remain quiet in trust, focused on your true desire, and you will sail through the thinking mind's tortures on the wings of faith in truth.

NTI Revelation, Chapter 20

(v 1 – 3) This is something you must be willing to do:

You must be willing to rest the thinking mind at every opportunity given you.

Learn to recognize your opportunities to rest the thinking mind. When you feel to go into prayer, rest and let a prayer rise from the Heart. When you feel to answer a question in the mind, rest and let the answer find its way into your awareness. When you feel tired and unsure as to what to do, rest and let a feeling of what to do enter you. When you feel inclined to speak and don't know what to say, rest and let what to say be given. And when you feel upset or saddened or afraid, rest and let illusions fade.

(v 4 – 6) When the thinking mind is rested, the Vision of Spirit is given. This Vision may guide you in all you think or do or say, because this Vision is your Vision based on the realization of true perception. This Vision knows the false as false and the true as true, so this Vision knows that which it sees. Knowing what it sees, it knows how to interact with it. And the purpose of each interaction is the purpose of awakening the one from the dream.

(v 7 – 10) Peaceful dreams end in peace. For one who has seen the peaceful purpose of awakening cannot see fear in dreams. The purpose is the same and has not changed, but this one can see it now. This one can see it now, because this one has learned to remember who he always is.

📖(v 11 – 15) *"Death and Hades were thrown into the lake of fire. This is the second death."*

When one chooses to let go of dreams, one chooses to let go of the ideas of dreams forever. The ideas of dreams are never real, but they are experienced as real as long as they are desired. When they are no longer desired, they cannot be experienced. They cease to be, no longer an idea in the mind, forever.

NTI Revelation, Chapter 21

📖(v 1) Then I saw a new heaven and a new earth, for the old heaven and the old earth had passed away, and there was no longer any division.

📖(v 2 - 4) And I saw the holy city of Jerusalem within my mind. Through this knowledge and this seeing, I saw all that I could not see before. I saw that I am in God and God is in me, and separation of the two is impossible. I saw that God is in my brothers and my brothers are in me, and separation and division are impossible. All that I had seen before, which caused me pain and suffering and loneliness, were wiped out forever. Before me, I saw only the expression of perfect freedom, and I knew that what I saw was Love.

(v 5) This is written down as a promise to all of mankind. Each one shall come to know this Vision and no one shall be left out. For this Vision is the reflection of your truth, and your truth is still in you.

(v 6 – 8) He who is thirsty, let him drink of the Wisdom of the Holy Spirit. Let Him teach you. Follow His guidance in trust and expectation that you shall be healed.

You are the free Son of God. Nothing can stand between you and your one true desire except your own desire to not know your Self.

You are free.

(v 9 – 14) Symbolism is gone forever when you can look beyond the symbols to the truth that merely *is*. In this truth do all symbols disappear, for in this truth is all interpretation rendered meaningless.

(v 15 – 21) That which cannot be described is indescribable, but it shall be known, because it is known. It is your truth, and it is within your knowing now. You need only to let go of everything that is not this knowing, without clinging to anything that feels safe within the familiar, and the familiar will fade away, that the *known* may shine within your mind. And there will be no words unless they are given you.

(v 22 – 27) All that is, all that ever was and all that is to come, is You. You are the Light and the vessel through which the Light shines. You are the reflection, which is made of your Light. You are all that is and separate from none of it. For there is only one, and since you *are*, you are the One.

NTI Revelation, Chapter 22

📖(v 1, 2) Then the angel showed me the water of the river of Life, clear as crystal, flowing from God and through God, and I was not apart from its flow. I was within its flow, and I was a part of its flow, and its flow came from me. I saw that the flow which comes from God is everything, and all that *is* is a part of its flow.

The tree of life is symbolic of the eternity that is. No one must eat from the tree of life or sit within its shade in order to gain eternal life. Eternal life already is and always has been, for this is the truth of Life. The tree of life never dies and never changes, although its leaves dance in the wind. This is the symbol of creation, and creation is what you are.

(v 3 – 6) When your eyes are opened, they shall not close again. For when you see, you will not choose to forget what you have seen. These words are trustworthy and true.

Only the truth is true. All else is illusion.

(v 7 - 9) What does it mean to worship God? It means to be grateful for all that you are and to seek no change from it.

(v 10, 11) Seek not to change that which you see, for that is to desire that *you* be different. Accept all that you see in glory and rejoicing, for that which you see is the mark of Heaven.

Do not worry that the mark is not the mark that you expect. Accept it *is* from Heaven, and you shall learn to see the mark differently.

📖(v 12, 13) "Behold, I am coming soon," is only a reminder. When you have forgotten and become lost within an image of what you are not, remember this statement and choose to see clearly again.

Everyone experiences according to his choice,
because you are the one who chooses.

(v 14, 15) Inside the inner chamber of your Heart you shall find and know your truth. It is not foreign to you. It is all that you are.

When you seem locked outside the light of the Heart, do not fear to choose again. Rest and trust that your Heart beckons to you. As you listen, you shall be drawn to it. As you listen, it shall come to you.

(v 16) Your truth is your foundation. And in your foundation, you find your strength. Let all else fade away, and a new house shall be built from the true foundation of Light.

(v 17) Come! The call is within you and the door is open. Come, and thirst no more. Come, and see that you *are* the river of Life.

(v 18, 19) Put aside all fear and listen only to the Voice of Love. Recognize your true Voice and follow it to the recognition of You.

(v 20, 21) *He who listens will surely hear.*
He who comes will know.
All will come, as none are to be left out.
This is the Word of God.
Amen.

Closing

I was asked to put together an abridged version of NTI that would help introduce NTI to people who are not familiar with it. I selected "the keys to NTI," the chapters that I have most often heard called "my favorite chapter" by students of NTI. These chapters are a good sampling of NTI's teaching and how that teaching is presented. If you found that these chapters did not appeal to you, you probably would not be attracted to NTI as a whole. I recommend following your heart in choosing your next book to read.

However, if these chapters did resonate with you, you may be interested in looking at "The Holy Spirit's Interpretation of the New Testament: A Course in Understanding and Acceptance" (NTI) as a full and complete course that points to truth.

NTI is made up of 27 primary chapters plus an introduction and an extensive question & answer index. This abridged version includes only a small portion of the total work. Here is a sample of the type of teaching you will find in other NTI chapters:

NTI John – Emphasizes that all people are the same and all people have the Light of God within them.

NTI Romans – Helps the reader see the metaphysical link between judgment and the continuation of illusion. Also helps the reader to see how acceptance is helpful to awakening.

NTI 2 Corinthians – Teaches the true concept of cause and effect; that is, cause is in the mind and the world is its effect.

NTI Ephesians – Teaches the law of Love, which is the law of mind or the law of thought. Shows how oneness is all that is and how oneness is in perfect operation now, even within the illusion of separation.

NTI Philippians – Teaches the reader how to ensure that one's motive is placed in harmony with one's faith, so that one is leading his/herself consistently toward the experience of enlightenment.

There is more, but since I am limited to a specific number of pages in this abridged version, I can't list every chapter and its purpose. Hopefully this additional sampling is helping you realize if NTI is for you. NTI is somewhat like a spiral staircase. It begins in the first chapter by teaching on a specific step, and it continually ascends from there. It is a course in understanding and acceptance. Like many courses, NTI builds upon the principles that it teaches as it moves through its 27 chapters. NTI is an interpretation that is much like an interpretative dance. Sometimes the interpretation sticks close to that which is being interpreted. Other times it spins off into a freer interpretation in order to carry the reader to a new place of understanding. The purpose of NTI is awakening to Self, and this purpose is the only focus throughout the interpretation.

If you are interested in continuing with NTI, there are two forms to choose from. You can read NTI or listen to it.

The book - Purchase the book, published by O-Books of London, from www.amazon.com or other book sellers.

The audio - For listening, you have two choices.
(1) You can purchase the book on CDs at www.diamondclearvision.com.
(2) Or you can download the book on mp3 from www.audiblespirit.com.

Regardless of what you decide, thank you for giving NTI a try.
Sincerely, Regina Dawn Akers (scribe and 1st student).